Learning with Digital Gan

Written for Higher Education teaching and learning professionals, *Learning with Digital Games* provides an accessible, straightforward introduction to the field of computer game-based learning. Up-to-date with current trends and the changing learning needs of today's students, this text offers friendly guidance, and is unique in its focus on post-school education and its pragmatic view of the use of computer games with adults.

Learning with Digital Games enables readers to quickly grasp practical and technological concepts, using examples that can easily be applied to their own teaching. The book assumes no prior technical knowledge but guides the reader step-by-step through the theoretical, practical and technical considerations of using digital games for learning. Activities throughout guide the reader through the process of designing a game for their own practice, and the book also offers:

- A toolkit of guidelines, templates and checklists
- Concrete examples of different types of game-based learning using six case studies
- Examples of games that show active and experiential learning
- Practical examples of educational game design and development

This professional guide upholds the sound reputation of the Open and Flexible Learning Series, is grounded in theory and closely links examples from practice. Higher Education academics, e-learning practitioners, developers and training professionals at all technical skill levels and experience will find this text is the perfect resource for explaining 'how to' integrate computer games into their teaching practice.

A companion website is available and provides up-to-date technological information, additional resources and further examples.

Nicola Whitton is a Research Fellow in the Education and Social Research Institute at Manchester Metropolitan University. Her website for *Learning with Digital Games* can be found at http://digitalgames.playthinklearn.net/

Open and Flexible Learning Series

Series Editors: Fred Lockwood, A.W. (Tony) Bates
and Som Naidu

Supporting Students in Online, Open and Distance Learning
2nd Edition
Ormond Simpson

Teaching with Audio in Open and Distance Learning
Derek Rowntree

Teaching Through Projects
Jane Henry

Towards More Effective Open and Distance Learning
Perc Marland

Understanding Learners in Open and Distance Education
Terry Evans

Using Communications Media in Open and Flexible Learning
Robin Mason

The Virtual University
Steve Ryan, Bernard Scott, Howard Freeman and Daxa Pate

Learning with Digital Games

A Practical Guide to Engaging Students in Higher Education

Nicola Whitton

Routledge
Taylor & Francis Group

NEW YORK AND LONDON

First published 2010
by Routledge
270 Madison Ave, New York, NY 10016

Simultaneously published in the UK
by Routledge
2 Park Square, Milton Park, Abingdon, Oxon OX14 4RN

Routledge is an imprint of the Taylor & Francis Group, an informa business

© 2010 Taylor and Francis

Typeset in Minion by
HWA Text and Data Management, London
Printed and bound in the United States of America on acid-free paper by
Walsworth Publishing Company, Marceline, MO

Library of Congress Cataloging in Publication Data
Whitton, Nicola.
    Learning with digital games : a practical guide to engaging students in higher
    education / by Nicola Whitton.
        p. cm. – (The open and flexible learning series)
    Includes bibliographical references and index.
    1. Education, Higher – Computer-assisted instruction. 2. Computer games.
    3. Educational games. I. Title.
    LB2395.7.W55 2009
    378.1'7370285–dc22   2009005748

ISBN 10: 0–415–99774–7 (hbk)
ISBN 10: 0–415–99775–5 (pbk)
ISBN 10: 0–203–87298–3 (ebk)

ISBN 13: 978–0–415–99774–4 (hbk)
ISBN 13: 978–0–415–99775–1 (pbk)
ISBN 13: 978–0–203–87298–7 (ebk)

To Alison Crerar, with grateful thanks for your mentorship, without which this book would never have been written.

Contents

Series Editor's Foreword

If there was any doubt about the popularity of computer games and their potential use in education, then a consideration of their sales and sums involved will dispel any doubt. Similarly, any visit to a household, or chat with friends and colleagues, will confirm the penetration of digital games into the home – and the hours of dedicated interaction by players.

In 2008, in the UK and the USA, the sale of computer games increased by over 40 and 20 per cent respectively, and achieved sales of £4.64 billion in the UK and $32 billion in the USA. In both countries, sales of digital games were higher than music CDs and videos combined. In the same year, Nintendo launched its new *Wii* Games Console in the USA and sold 600,000 units in the first eight days; Nintendo estimates sales of 50 million units by March 2009. This is in addition to the sales of the other two game providers – Microsoft's Xbox and Sony's PlayStation 3. This represents an impressive take-up of the technology and application.

In contrast, higher education institutions have been slow to explore and exploit the potential of such digital games – despite the massive investment in communication and information technology. For many in higher education the focus of digital games on entertainment rather than education, and a focus on low-level conceptual skills in educational gaming, are often cited as reasons why such games are of limited value. (However, you will discover that Nicola argues, and provides evidence, that educational applications are both possible and effective and that higher levels skills can be deployed within such games.) Educationalists also argue that the sophisticated technical skills required of those constructing the games, and enormous development costs, makes their use prohibitive in higher education. Whilst Nicola acknowledges these points she does provide advice, assistance and resources that can mitigate their constraints. Certainly, this book, *Learning with Digital Games: A Practical Guide to Engaging Students in Higher Education* by Nicola Whitton, not only gives us access to the world of digital games but the tools and frameworks to become part of it.

Nicola provides a sound rationale for the inclusion of digital games into the repertoire of teachers in higher education. She draws upon her own research in the field, and knowledge of it, in presenting an insight into the theory, practice and technology associated with this world. In the past, you may have found those steeped in a particular academic area to be dismissive of the problems that novices face or evangelical in their claims – not Nicola. She is realistic – it is reassuring to hear her say that 'games are not necessarily an appropriate way of teaching everything' – and pragmatic in her approach. She bases her arguments on sound educational principles and supplements these with practical advice and concrete examples, criteria against which you can judge the development of digital games and activities and which will enable you to create your own. What I particularly like about the book is that throughout, Nicola stresses the importance of clear learning objectives, activities to realize these coupled with assessment of the learning outcomes. The supplementary website promises to be a unique source of help and information.

This book has certainly encouraged me to reassess some of the 'paper-based' games I have developed as well as motivating me to think of new applications in my teaching. I am sure it will do the same for you – contributing to your teaching and to student learning.

Fred Lockwood
Yelvertoft, February 2009

Acknowledgements

I would like to thank everyone who has provided me with support and advice during the writing of this book. In particular Fred Lockwood, whose guidance has been invaluable, and Sue Beasley, Thomas Hainey, Hanno Hildmann and Paul Hollins for their insights and feedback.

I am especially grateful to the people who have contributed case studies and shared their experiences: Chris Goldsmith, Richard Hall, Niki Hynes, John Pal, Katie Piatt, Mark Stubbs, David White and Elisabeth Yaneske.

I would also like to thank everyone who has kindly helped me to secure permission to use the screen shots that feature throughout this book, in particular Bart Bonte, Robert Firebaugh, Nora Herron, Andreas Holzinger, Martin Kerstein, Martin Klima, Jobe Makar, David Münnich, Cathy Orr, Terri Perkins, Elias Pimenidis, Leslie Rosenthal, Ben Ringold, Adam Tuckwell and Robert Wahlstedt.

Finally, I would like to offer my very grateful thanks to my long-suffering husband, Peter, who, through his unwavering support and sound advice, has somehow managed to keep me sane over the past year.

CHAPTER 1

Introduction

Learning with Digital Games: A Practical Guide to Engaging Students in Higher Education aims to provide a straightforward introduction to the creation and use of computer games to support learning, teaching and assessment with adult learners. It is aimed at anyone with an interest in the use of digital games to enhance teaching, and does not assume a high prior level of technical knowledge, but will take the reader step by step through the design and development processes required to incorporate digital games within higher education. I hope that this text will offer a friendly and accessible introduction to the area, providing inspiration and ideas as well as practical guidance.

I have worked for many years as a developer, teacher and researcher in the field of technology-enhanced learning, with a particular interest in collaborative computer game-based learning. This book is based around the work carried out for my doctoral thesis, 'An investigation into the potential of collaborative computer game-based learning in higher education' (Whitton, 2007). In this volume, my research and experience has been distilled into the lessons learned from this work, with supporting activities to enable the reader to understand the theoretical context, address the practical considerations of using games for learning and consider the best ways in which to implement digital games for learning in your own subject discipline. Throughout I have aimed to keep this book practical in nature, providing advice on the application of digital games in teaching and learning with tips, guidelines, checklists and short case studies.

In the first part of this introductory chapter I explain and discuss the background to the creation of this book, explore the rationale for a book aimed specifically at using computer games with learners in higher education (as opposed to school-aged learners or in the context of training) and describe the structure of the book and the elements that are contained within it. The second half of the chapter provides some examples from the game-based learning literature of ways in which games have been used in this arena, and aims to provide some initial ideas of the scope and applicability of the medium. I hope that after reading this chapter you will begin to see the potential of digital games for learning and will be enthused to think about ways in which the principles discussed here might apply to your own situations.

Background to the Book

The primary objective of this book is to offer a practical starting point for anyone who is interested in the use of computer games for learning within the higher education context. It is not limited to online games used at a distance, a common conception of computer games for learning, but includes the use of games in a range of environments and circumstances, from face-to-face in traditional classroom settings to online virtual worlds, and draws upon a range of game genres that I feel are particularly appropriate for supporting learning at this level.

Learning with Digital Games is aimed at anyone with an interest in games and education, including lecturers, educational developers, e-learning practitioners and researchers. It provides theory to underpin the practical advice and examples provided, though I have tried not to be heavily theoretical – the aim is to allow individuals to apply the principles of game-based learning with technology to improve the student experience.

Although this book draws together pedagogic, practical and technological aspects of learning with digital games, it is not expected that the reader will become an expert in the theories of learning, or a technical mastermind (and a high level of technical expertise is not required to follow the narrative or complete the activities) but will, however, gain the ability to start to consider how to appropriately use the techniques suggested. The pedagogy that underpins the use of technology is central to the ethos of this book and I hope that after reading it, and completing the suggested activities, you will be filled with ideas about different approaches to adopt to make the best use of digital games to enhance teaching, learning and assessment.

This book also aims to provide sound advice and ideas on how to apply digital games to real teaching and learning contexts, based on robust research evidence. It is worth saying up front that at the current time this evidence is somewhat limited in the area of higher education, although several good examples do exist and I hope that the research and evidence base will grow over time. Therefore, while the examples provided in this book are predominantly based in the higher education sphere, I will at times draw on examples and evidence from children's education, further education, informal learning, training and adult learning in other contexts, where this is appropriate and transferable. Likewise, the techniques and tools provided in the book can also be applied to a similar range of contexts (bearing in mind the differences between learners in higher education and other areas, as discussed in Chapter 3) and I hope that this book will also be of interest to practitioners in these related areas. My own experience is primarily in the UK higher education context, and the majority of the examples and case studies used in this book come from this environment. However, where possible, I have tried to include examples from other spheres, and highlighted differences that may impact on how they may be applied.

Learning with Digital Games is unashamedly written from a constructivist learning perspective, taking the underlying philosophical approach that students learn actively by doing things (rather than simply reading or being told about them), and construct their own conceptions of what they are learning, using other people as a way of testing and refining their understandings. While, undoubtedly there are examples of computer games used successfully in an instructional or transmissional model in higher education and in other educational areas, I feel that to understand the real potential of digital games it is best to view them as active learning environments, which have the potential to teach higher level skills such as analysis, application and evaluation (Bloom, 1956) and this is the predominant focus here.

It is worth making the point early on that the reader should recognize that the advice provided in this book, although based on sound evidence and experience, will not apply in every learning and teaching situation. It is crucial to apply the principles described here with discretion and creativity and adapt the use of digital games to the student group, the skills and experience of the teacher, and the nature of the subject area. What this book does aim to provide is the pedagogic understanding and background to help the reader use computer games appropriately in a given situation (or decide that there are alternative, preferable ways to teach or learn).

There are several ways to approach how you use this book: it may be read start-to-finish to provide an introductory overview to the use of digital game-based learning in higher education; you may also choose to work through the activities provided in each chapter as a starting point. It can also be employed as a reference tool or practical manual for the reader to dip into particular areas of interest or research certain topics as and when the need arises. I have included activities throughout, which will take the reader through the process of specifying, designing and obtaining appropriate games for learning in their own contexts, and provide the opportunity to apply the principles described.

In this book I have aimed to cover all the bases concerning the background to digital game-based learning, splitting the main body of the book into three parts, and looking first at the pedagogic theory, then the application in practice, then the technologies that can be used. On its own, each of these parts also provides an introduction to its respective area, so each can also be seen as stand-alone. I wanted this book to be used as an easily accessible reference, so at the end of each chapter there is a summary of the important points covered in that chapter. I have also tried to contextualize the points that I make in this book as far as possible and use examples and case studies throughout; more detailed examples in the form of extended case studies are also available on the website that accompanies this book.

In my opinion a book that concentrates predominantly on the use of digital games with learners in higher education is needed because, while there are several other excellent books in the area, they tend to focus on the use of games with children, or focus on learning in the context of training, which I feel misses some of the great potential of the field for supporting active and contextualized learning. In the section that follows I will discuss the rationale for thinking about digital games for learning in the context of higher education differently from that in other, more widely explored, areas.

The Higher Education Context

While there have been several excellent books published in recent years that look at the potential of computer game-based learning, in general, these books tend to focus on children's learning and, where adult learning is considered, they tend to be skills-focused, training-related or based around memorization of facts. From my own background as a teacher and educational developer in higher education and a researcher in digital games for learning, I feel that many of the arguments that are made for the use of games with these groups do not always directly transfer to students in higher education and that by focusing on these areas we are not exploring the real potential of digital games.

I believe that there is a great deal that can be learned from other educational fields, including further education, the schools sector, and the commercial and training sectors (and vice versa that much of this book can be applied in these areas), but that an understanding of the differences is important to be able to make informed decisions about how games should be used and what is appropriate in a given context. From my perspective, there are a number of fundamental differences in the ways in which it is appropriate to use games with children, or in drill-and-practice situations, as opposed to the higher level learning that takes place at university, and these are shown in the box opposite.

A concept that I would like to discuss early on, and one that I can safely say is not a premise behind my enthusiasm for computer games for learning, is the notion of the 'games generation', 'digital natives' (Prensky, 2001, 2006) or 'net generation' (Oblinger, 2004). These terms are all used to express the hypothesis

Acceptability

The way in which the concepts of play and fun are perceived during learning differs in higher education. While they might be seen as appropriate elements within the context of children's learning, games are perceived by many learners and teachers in higher education as frivolous and a distraction. Perceptions of the appropriateness of games will affect the degree to which they are seen as acceptable by their users, so a greater emphasis on the purposefulness of games and on their pedagogic rationale is required in this context.

Applicability to the real world

Learners in higher education, and adult learners in general, are more likely to need to see the real-world relevance of what they are learning and be able to transfer what they have learned into authentic contexts. This has implications for the design of games and their supporting activities outside the game environment.

Assessment

The assessment of digital games for learning is one of the key issues that this book aims to address, and whether or not a game is assessed will affect the dynamic of its use and the engagement of learners. Lecturers in higher education also have a great deal more flexibility in the way in which courses are assessed than teachers in schools, and it is this freedom that creates greater potential for the integration of effective digital game-based learning, while at the same time raising questions about the types of assessment that are appropriate at this level.

Cognitive level of learning outcomes

The nature of the learning outcomes at university level (particularly at the end of an undergraduate degree and in postgraduate studies) do not focus simply on memorization, repetition of facts or understanding of a topic. Instead, they tend to focus on higher level cognitive outcomes, looking at skills such as critical thinking, evaluation, synthesis and application, and the types of computer game that are appropriate in this context are different from those used to teach lower-level skills.

continued

Motivation

The motivations of adults, both to undertake learning and to engage in game-based learning are different from those of younger learners. Adults have a range of different reasons for taking part in learning and choose to engage voluntarily in the higher education system. Computer games are often justified in education on the grounds that they are 'motivational', but in my experience this is not necessarily the case for adults (and certainly not all adults). A rationale for the use of games simply as motivational tools is not appropriate in higher education and is an oversimplification of the motivations that surround adult engagement in learning.

Orientation to study

Students in higher education are required to take a greater responsibility for their own learning, have a greater understanding of the learning process itself and develop more mature and self-reflective attitudes to learning. Concepts such as 'stealth learning' that have been applied to games, where learners learn by playing a game without necessarily understanding what or how they are learning, are not appropriate to this context.

that exposure to technology from an early age has changed the way in which young people (i.e. our current generation of students) think and approach technology. Prensky (2001) describes a definite distinction between 'digital natives' who have grown up with computer games, television and other media, and use them to learn instinctively, and older learners, for whom interacting with these types of technology has to be done through conscious effort. He argues that the generation of people brought up in a world of computers (the majority of our current generation of students) are cognitively different from previous generations and that this immersion in technology has fundamentally changed the way in which people acquire and assimilate information.

This idea is still commonly used as an argument for the use of games in education, although it is now generally thought, by educationalists, to be flawed. I very strongly feel that labelling whole generational groups in this way is not helpful and, indeed, self-limiting – particularly in relation to terms such as 'digital divide' or 'generation gap', which imply that any difference is insurmountable (and serves only to highlight differences rather than focusing on commonality). While it is can be useful to highlight that differences do exist, it is important to realize that the situation is more complex than simply two ways of being (e.g. *natives* and *immigrants*) and that individual approaches to technology and information are not necessarily fixed. Bennett and colleagues (2008) argue, from a recent analysis of the literature on digital natives, that the relationship between young people and technology is more complex and that there is no evidence of generationally different learning styles. They call for a more measured and rigorous research approach, with a plea for a 'considered and rigorous investigation that includes the perspectives of young people and their teachers, and genuinely seeks to understand the situation before proclaiming the need for widespread change' (Bennett *et al.*, 2008: 784).

From my own experience it is factors such as the level and time of exposure to the technology that affect learners' (and teachers') confidence in using it, and alter the ways in which all people interact with and use computers. I can certainly think of older individuals who are far more attuned to using computers than some other individuals in their teens, and feel that there is no reason to assume, just because an individual is confident using computers, that he or she would desire to use them as a method of learning or instinctively knows how to use them effectively in that context. Two recent UK studies provide evidence that students may not be as comfortable with technology for learning and new ways of working as is commonly assumed. In a study of student expectations of higher education, IPSOS MORI (2007) found that while the group of potential students who took part in their study had grown up with technology they did not value the use of technology for its own sake, but instead put a high value on face-to-face teaching and traditional teacher–student interaction. A recent study by CIBER (2008) also provides evidence that the assumption that young people who are brought up in the information age are more web-literate than older people is false. Although young people show an apparent ease with computers, they rely heavily on search engines and lack critical and analytic skills. In fact, the study claims, character traits that are often associated with young web users, such as lack of tolerance of delay in search and navigation, are actually true of all age groups of web users.

In relation to learning in higher education it is also important to recognize that as technology becomes increasingly pervasive, *all learners* will adapt the ways they interact with computers, and that we cannot make sweeping assumptions about a particular generation, or any group of learners. Instead we should cater for all degrees of technical competence and confidence, and accept that many people (of all ages) will simply prefer to communicate, play and learn in ways that are not associated with technology.

Throughout this book I will argue that digital game-based learning is not a simple solution that is going to revolutionize teaching and learning in higher education by appealing to a new 'generation' of learners, nor is it going to appeal to every student in every situation. I think it is important that digital games are seen as simply another tool available to lecturers and teachers, which, when considered and implemented with regard to the constraints of the higher education system and appropriate pedagogic models, can provide an effective and engaging way to learn.

Structure of the Book

Following this introductory chapter, the main body of this book is made up of three parts: Theory, Practice and Technology. I then present six case studies detailing the effective use of digital games for learning in different higher education institutions, written by expert practitioners in the field. The book concludes with a final chapter drawing together the themes of the book, highlighting the key lessons, and considering future areas of research. The first part, Theory, provides a context and background to the use of digital games for learning in higher education to underpin the later parts of the book. The second part, Practice, looks at the use of digital games in real teaching and learning situations, and provides lots of tips and advice on how to start thinking about their use in your own area. The third part, Technology, focuses on the game, development software and platforms available and provides a grounding for the reader in the different options that are available for finding (or developing) the type of game required. The final chapter of the book, Conclusions, takes a holistic look at what has been discussed throughout and considers the challenges for digital game-based learning in higher education, as well as discussing future areas for research.

Each of the core parts of the book has three chapters, and all nine chapters include a number of elements to help you navigate their content and easily find the information you are looking for. Every chapter starts with a clear *chapter overview*, which briefly summarizes what you can expect to learn by reading the chapter and undertaking the activities within it. There are a number of *activities* spread throughout each chapter, which are entirely optional, but provide a way to relate the content discussed in the chapter to your own learning and teaching practice, if desired. By undertaking the activities you will be able to work through the process of identifying which types of game may be most appropriate in your own situation, considering the practical implications and constraints, and identifying the appropriate technology to locate, modify or create the game itself.

In order to aid the use of this book for reference, in each chapter *key terms* will be highlighted and definitions can be found in the *glossary* at the end of the book. I have also provided a short *summary* at the end of each chapter as a quick overview of the main points made. In addition, many chapters contain a short list of *further reading* for anyone who is particularly interested in the topic. The following three subsections provide a short overview of each of the chapters in the three main parts in this book.

Theory

The first part of the book focuses on the theory of digital games and its relation to pedagogic theory. Chapter 2, 'Recognizing the Characteristics of Digital Games', presents the inclusive definition of *digital games* used throughout this book, drawing together a range of definitions from various fields and discussing the problems of creating a single exact description. The chapter also considers other game-like activities that exist and how they relate to the use of digital games for learning.

Chapter 3, 'Understanding the Pedagogy of Digital Games', provides an overview of the pedagogic potential of digital games and explores the rationale for using them to enhance teaching and learning in higher education. It first examines the ways in which adult learning differs from children's learning and, in particular, the influence this may have on motivations to learn with games. The chapter discusses the importance of engagement with learning and the pedagogic rationale for using computer games in higher education, drawing on constructivist theories of active learning, including collaborative learning, experiential learning and problem-based learning, and concludes by examining the nature of engagement with games.

The final chapter in this section on theory, Chapter 4, 'Identifying Types of Digital Game for Learning', examines the different types of digital game that are available to educators and the different ways in which they can be used to facilitate different types of learning. A taxonomy of game types is presented and discussed in relation to types of learning, again with a specific focus on learning in higher education. The chapter finishes by briefly discussing new directions in digital games for learning.

After reading this first part of the book, and undertaking the activities within it, the reader should possess a sound background knowledge of the range of theoretical issues associated with the pedagogy behind using digital games for learning, will understand why a pedagogical rationale is crucial for the use of digital games in the context of higher education, and will be able to identify types of game that might be appropriate in their own learning and teaching practice.

Practice

The second section of the book looks at the practice of using digital games to teach in higher education. Chapter 5, 'Integrating Digital Games Into the Curriculum', explores the context in which a digital game is to be used and a range of practical issues that need to be considered when integrating digital games into a higher education curriculum. Issues such as student expectations, learning to play the game and safety are highlighted. The chapter provides a technique for analysing teaching situations to assess the appropriateness of digital games and identify constraints that exist. The second half of the chapter considers the differences between working face-to-face and online and describes a number of different options for integrating computer game-based learning into teaching and learning.

Chapter 6, 'Designing a Digital Game for Learning', considers what is good practice in the design of games for learning, and how games, and their associated activities, can be designed to support the learning process. It first addresses a number of pedagogic design considerations, including the alignment of learning objectives and game activities, ways to support collaboration, and the development of associated activities. The different options for identifying or creating appropriate games are briefly discussed and a framework for developing a game design concept presented.

The final chapter in the section on practice, Chapter 7, 'Assessing the Impact of Digital Games on Learning', looks at two different ways in which the impact of digital game-based learning can be assessed. First, it looks at ways to integrate the game into the formal assessment for a course. Secondly, it looks at ways of carrying out research into the impact of a game, in terms of both learning and the wider student experience. Ways in which to evaluate the student experience are discussed and a model is presented for assessing student engagement with game-based learning.

After working through this part, the reader will have gained an insight into the spectrum of practical issues that need to be considered when implementing digital game-based learning in a higher education curriculum.

Technology

The third part of this book explores issues associated with the technology of digital games. Chapter 8, 'Using Existing Digital Games for Learning', explores the potential of using existing commercial entertainment and educational games for learning, considering first the benefits and disadvantages of this approach, and discussing the design differences between entertainment and educational games. The chapter also looks at the potential for using multi-user virtual worlds and modifying existing gaming environments for learning. A number of web resources for obtaining games for learning are also presented.

Chapter 9, 'Developing New Digital Games for Learning', focuses on the technology to support the creation of new games, again beginning with a discussion of the pros and cons of the approach. It then goes on to describe the range of skills required to develop an educational game from first principles. The process of developing a functional specification to support game development is considered and, finally, a range of development tools that are available for game creation are presented.

The final chapter in the technology section, Chapter 10, 'Evaluating Digital Games for Learning', looks at ways in which to evaluate the usability, accessibility and potential educational value of digital games. It provides a brief overview of the principles of user-centred design and discusses the value of prototyping and user testing. Guidelines are also presented to support the design of games that are effective for learning and are accessible, usable and easy to learn.

After reading this part, and completing the associated activities, readers will have an understanding of the technical issues involved in the use and development of educational game, as well as an idea about the technological options available. It is intrinsic to the nature of gaming technology to be fast moving and therefore to date quickly, so as far as possible, I have aimed not to discuss specific versions of technologies, applications or platforms. However, a wide range of further details and links are available on the companion website (described in the section below).

Case Studies and Conclusion

In addition to the three main parts, the book also contains six case studies, contributed by leading academics and practitioners in the field of learning with digital games. These provide a real-life insight into how computer games can be used in practice and draw out themes that have been encountered throughout the book.

At the end of the book a short concluding chapter brings together some of the themes and ideas that have arisen, and explores some of the challenges of game-based learning in the coming years. It is my aim that by having completed the activities that occur throughout the book the reader will be at the point of having specified an appropriate game for his or her teaching situation, and have developed strategies for obtaining or creating the game, ways of embedding it appropriately within the curriculum, and identified techniques for assessing its value.

Web Resources to Accompany the Book

Learning with Digital Games is accompanied by a companion website, which is available at http://digitalgames.playthinklearn.net/ and contains a range of resources to complement the content and activities in the book. The fast-paced nature of the field means that published references to specific software or games are in danger of being out-of-date before the book is even published, therefore, this type of content will be included on the website rather than in the book itself to enable it to stay current.

The website contains five sections:

* *Supporting materials* for each chapter, which contains links to all the resources, readings and tools mentioned, as well as online versions of the

activities, screenshots and digital versions of any forms or checklists that were provided in the chapter.

- *Games* contains links to all the games referenced or described in the book, as well as other games that are relevant or of interest.
- *Resources* contains links to additional publications, development tools and websites that are relevant to the field of learning with digital games.
- *Case studies* contains versions of each of the case studies that are included in the book.
- *Feedback* provides the opportunity for you to tell me what you think of the book as well as the website itself, and suggest additional resources, games or case studies. I very much value any comments or opinions readers would like to offer.

Activity: Familiarizing yourself with the companion website

Take ten or fifteen minutes now to go online and have a look at what the companion website has to offer. On the home page you will see links to the five main sections and from there you can navigate simply to any of the areas described above.

Examples Used throughout the Book

This book is intended to be as accessible as possible, so I am making no assumptions as to your prior experiences of playing games. I thought it worthwhile therefore to provide three examples that I refer to throughout the book, which are freely available online for you to play and will allow you get a feel for some of the concepts I will refer to. These examples are used extensively in the early activities but, of course, if you are already familiar with a range of different types of game feel free to use ones you already know.

The three games that I have selected have been chosen because I think they provide good examples of different genres of game and some of the points I want to raise throughout the book, they are available online so are easily accessible and will run on a variety of platforms, and they all have some potential for learning (and, of course, I think that they're fun).

These examples selected are not necessarily the finest examples of the genre, nor do they have the highest production values or exemplify all of the points of good design of educational games (these games are, after all, designed for entertainment, not for learning). However, these games are easy to start playing and show a good range of game design features that exemplify many of the principles that I discuss throughout the book.

RuneScape is an online multi-user fantasy role-playing game in which the player can navigate around and interact with the environment, objects and other

Figure 1.1 *RuneScape* (image reproduced with permission of Jagex Ltd)

players in order to solve quests and progress through the game. RuneScape (see Figure 1.1) provides a good example of a complex game that is relatively easy to learn, creates opportunities for collaboration with other players and provides a vast interactive world to explore.

NotPron is a single-player puzzle game, which describes itself as 'the hardest riddle available on the internet' and consists of a series of puzzles of increasing difficulty that the player has to solve to progress through different levels of the game (see Figure 1.2). Although the puzzles do become hard relatively quickly (and require an increasing degree of technical know-how) I think this provides an excellent example of a game that uses simple technology to create engaging game-play.

Sleuth is an online detective game where the player has to solve mysteries by searching locations for clues, gathering evidence and talking to suspects in order to solve a number of cases that gradually increase in difficulty (see Figure 1.3). I have chosen this game because it provides a good example of a detailed environment and objects that the player can interact with in order to make logical deductions about the case.

Figure 1.2 *NotPron* (image reproduced with permission of David Münnich)

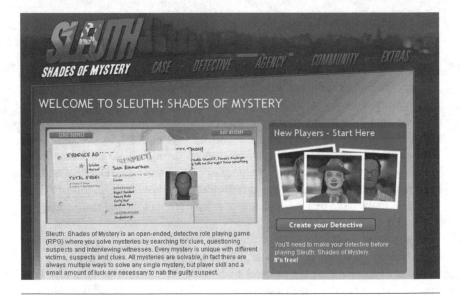

Figure 1.3 *Sleuth* (image reproduced with permission of Hypothetical Software)

Activity: Familiarizing yourself with the games

These three games will be used as examples throughout the book, so this example simply involves familiarizing yourself with each of them. You can find the web sites for each of the games on the companion website or navigate there directly using the web addresses below. Spend 15–20 minutes initially on each game (or longer if you like) simply getting a feel for the interface, the type of game play that is involved and what is expected of you as a player.

RuneScape and *Sleuth* will require you to register before you can play but this should be straightforward. Don't worry if you find *NotPron* tricky at first – you have to think laterally – and you can always use the hints provided and the help forums (there's a link at the bottom of each page).

RuneScape can be accessed at http://www.runescape.com – have a go at working through the tutorial. *NotPron* can be found at http://www.notpron. com – see how many levels you can progress through (you should be easily able to manage the first three). *Sleuth* is available at http://www.playsleuth. com – see if you can solve the first case.

Don't worry if you find any of these games difficult to start playing or get engaged with (particularly if you are new to playing computer games) – I've selected three very different games so they are unlikely to all appeal to everyone. If you get really stuck then I've provided some hints on the companion website that should help you (or just move on for now – it is not my aim to make you play games you hate, more to get a feel for different types of game and what they can offer).

I hope that by spending some time playing these games you will now have a feel (particularly if you don't regularly play computer games) for three different genres and the types of gaming interface that exist (and possibly the frustrations that your students may feel getting started). This will provide you with a context for thinking about the issues presented as the book progresses.

PART I

Theory

CHAPTER 2

Recognizing the Characteristics of Digital Games

This chapter provides an inclusive working definition of digital games for learning and considers other activities that are like games and apply many of the same principles.

I discuss first my conception of the term *digital games for learning*. I show how this definition came about by drawing on the views of researchers and practitioners in the field, and consider other 'game-like' activities in relation to education. In the final section I discuss the ways in which game characteristics can be applied to learning.

Defining Digital Games for Learning

As the starting point for this book I thought it would be useful to discuss exactly what I mean by *digital games* in this context. I'll start with the relatively easy *digital* part and then move on to the more complex issue of how to define what a *game* is. This is hampered by the fact that there is no single accepted definition of what a *game* itself might be – definitions depend very much on the discipline and background of the individuals creating them; for example, footballers, mathematicians, computer programmers and psychologists may all have very different views on how to describe a *game*. I don't want to dwell in too much detail on what is essentially a semantic point, nor do I wish to recover ground that many others have looked at in far greater detail, but I do think it is important for the reader to understand the extent of the types of activities I include in this book.

So, to get the straightforward part out of the way, by *digital* I mean using an electronic device of some kind, either online or stand-alone. This includes desktop computers, laptop computers, game consoles, handheld devices, mobile phones, digital audio players, mobile game consoles and so on. I am essentially interested in anything with a microchip capable of playing a game (if my washing machine could play games, I would include it here). In the context of this book, the *digital* element can be integral to the game, or a peripheral part of a larger game-play scenario (e.g. a game that takes place predominantly offline where strategies are discussed in online forums).

In terms of my own research, I struggled for some time trying to find an appropriate definition of a game; initially so that I could make a distinction between different types of activities and identify those that are, by definition, games and those that are not. Unfortunately, I soon discovered that it isn't possible to be so explicit – even in any single field few definitions exactly coincide. The concept of defining a *game* is one that has been troubling even philosophers for some time. Wittgenstein (1976) argued that it is impossible to have a single definition but that an exact classification is not necessary to be able to study games effectively. I agree with this in principle; however, for the purpose of this book I think it is still useful to be able to more accurately define what I mean by *game* in the context of learning in order to be able to look in more detail at the types of activities that are included.

In the sections that follow I will first look at some of the different ways in which researchers and practitioners in the field have defined games themselves and present my own framework of characteristics for defining games. I will then examine some of the other activities that are on the periphery of games (I include these other activities because I feel that, while not technically games in the view of some people, they still have a lot to offer education). The final section discusses how these characteristics of games relate to more traditional learning activities and can be applied to learning situations.

By thinking about your own conception of what a *game* is at this point, you will be able to see how your definition relates to the one presented later in the chapter.

Ways of Defining Games

When I first started thinking about exactly what sorts of activities could be considered to be games, I started by looking at the types of definitions that are used in three particular different areas of the gaming literature: game-based learning with traditional (i.e. non-digital) games; computer games for entertainment; and digital game-based learning.

Activity: Thinking About Your Own Definition of a Game

Take two minutes to quickly write down five activities that you consider to be games.

Using your list, take another five minutes to write down all the characteristics you can think of that these games share (e.g. if you've written *hockey*, *basketball* and *football* as games you might conclude that they are all played on pitches, have teams and some kind of referee or adjudicator).

Think now about each characteristic that you've written down: would you say it is an essential element of what makes an activity a game? Which of your characteristics would you use to form your own definition of games?

Write down your list of characteristics that you think define a game (you'll be referring back to it later).

My starting point was to look at the way in which traditional games have been defined, as there is a long history of games being used for learning. Ellington and colleagues (1982) define a game as simply having two characteristics: rules and competition (which can be either among players or against the game system itself). This seems like a sensible and straightforward definition; however, it is perhaps too basic to form a complete definition. In one of the seminal texts on games, Caillois (2001) defines four different types of games: those that involve competition (e.g. sports); those that involve chance (e.g. gambling); those that involve simulation (e.g. children's dressing-up games); and those that involve what he terms *vertigo*, such as fairground rides. It is notable that in these four types, competition is only included as a distinct element in one, and rules assumed (if implicitly) only in the first two. Also, games based around puzzle-solving do not neatly fit into this definition. Klabbers (1999) provides a definition that is typical among educationalists working with traditional games, saying that a game is 'an activity or sport involving skill, knowledge or chance, in which you follow fixed rules and try to win against an opponent to solve a puzzle' (Klabbers, 1999: 18).

Definitions from commercial game designers show a different perspective. Seminal game designer Chris Crawford (1984) argues that the elements that define a game are representation (being a formalized and fantastic version of reality), interaction (with other people or with the game itself), conflict or challenge, and the provision of a safe environment, one where the consequences of actions do not hold in reality. Other designers have included more intangible aspects such as *playability* and *fun* into their definitions. Oxland (2004) says that computer games are defined by rules and boundaries, feedback, an interface to the game world, context sensitivity, goals, quests and challenges, a game environment and playability, while Koster (2005) provides a much less detailed definition, saying simply that games are puzzles to solve, exercises for our brains. With a focus on entertainment, it is unsurprising that there is a greater focus on the user experience in the game designers' definitions described here.

As well as games theorists and designers, there are also definitions by researchers in the field of digital game-based learning specifically. Dempsey and colleagues (2002) define a game as an activity involving one or more players, with goals, constraints, payoffs and consequences, which is rule-guided, artificial in some respects and has an element of competition, while Prensky (2001) describes six structural elements of games: rules, goals, outcomes and feedback, competition or challenge, interaction, and representation or story. A wider definition is used by de Freitas who defines computer-based learning games as:

> applications using the characteristics of video and computer games to create engaging and immersive learning experiences for delivering specified learning goals, outcomes and experiences.
>
> (de Freitas, 2006: 9)

I find this characteristic-based definition one of the most useful because it is open and inclusive, as well as being specifically related to educational games. It is evident, even from this small snapshot of the literature that tries to define games, that there are many different ways to view games, and that the definitions seldom wholly coincide, although you will have probably noticed that there are many common characteristics. By focusing on these characteristics, rather than on a single definition that leads to a binary view of game/non-game, this allows a whole range of game-like activities to be included in the definition where they share characteristics with games. For the purpose of my research – and now this book – I wanted to use as inclusive a definition as possible, because many of the same learning principles apply whether you want to describe an activity as a *sport, simulation, interactive fiction, puzzle* or *game*.

An Inclusive Definition of Games

Considering the wide variety of definitions that occur in the literature, it seemed unhelpful and artificial – if not impossible – to create an absolute division of what is (and is not) a game. There is no single common definition and practitioners from different disciplines have different perspectives. I think that it is more useful to adopt an approach where the notion of a *game* is defined on the basis of key characteristics (but where it is accepted that not all games will necessarily exhibit all characteristics). This approach allows the inclusion and consideration of a range of game-like activities that are interesting in terms of their educational value, but might not be considered to be *truly* games by some.

Table 2.1 Ten Defining Characteristics of Games

Characteristic	Definition
Competition	The goal is to achieve an outcome that is superior to others.
Challenge	Tasks require effort and are non-trivial.
Exploration	There is a context-sensitive environment that can be investigated.
Fantasy	Existence of a make-believe environment, characters or narrative.
Goals	There are explicit aims and objectives.
Interaction	An action will change the state of play and generate feedback.
Outcomes	There are measurable results from game play (e.g. scoring).
People	Other individuals take part.
Rules	The activity is bounded by artificial constraints.
Safety	The activity has no consequence in the real world.

I have used the characteristics of games that commonly occur in definitions from the literature, aiming to provide an open definition of *game*, where activities can be considered to be *game-like* or *game-based* if they exhibit some of the characteristics (but not necessarily all, or even most). The more of these characteristics an activity possesses, the more essentially *game-like* it can be considered to be. From an analysis of definitions (including those mentioned), I identified ten defining characteristics of games, which are summarized in Table 2.1.

Competition

This exists where the aim of the activity is to *win* by achieving a better result than one or more other players. It is also possible for an individual to compete against themselves, for example beating a score that was achieved on a previous occasion. Some games involve competition in that they are played with other people in real time (e.g. a multi-player car racing game) while others allow competition with others playing at different times (e.g. an arcade game with a high score table). Games such as adventure games, where players have to solve a series of puzzles to complete the game, are not strictly competitive (using this definition), although they are certainly challenging (see the next point). It is possible to make almost any activity competitive by including an outcome that different people can measure their performance against (e.g. a run can be made competitive by timing it and comparing the time with those achieved by other people).

Challenge

This is the idea that a task has some degree of difficulty, is not trivial to complete and requires effort to achieve. Different games will have different degrees of challenge, from the simplistic to the highly complex, and the concept of challenge can be highly individual – what is highly challenging to one individual may be simple to another, and the degree of challenge in a multi-player game may also depend on the skill of the opponent. The type of challenge can take many forms, for example they can be mental (solving a puzzle), physical (climbing a wall) or social (negotiating a deal). Complex games such as role-playing games, where players take on the role of a character in a fantasy world and take part in quests, offer a range of challenges of different levels and types, while more simple games and puzzles may offer less in the way of challenge.

Exploration

This describes the concept that the activity takes place in a simulated environment – which can be real, virtual or imaginary – and that this environment can be explored by the player. There are places, objects and people to be discovered and interacted with and exploration of the environment stimulates curiosity as to what elements exist in the game world and how they can be used. The game environment can consist of actual locations (virtually or physically) or it can be the interface and the meta-environment of the game (e.g. exploration of the constraints of the game and discovering what controls are and what they do). For example, *RuneScape* (Figure 2.1) provides a massive virtual world with thousands of locations that the player can navigate around and explore, while *Sleuth* (Figure 2.2) has a more limited set of locations but the exploration of each scene and discovery of evidence takes place in much greater detail.

Fantasy

This is the element of make-believe underlying a game, including the creation of a fictional gaming environment, the narrative that holds together the action and the characters that inhabit the game world. The word fantasy – particularly in relation to games – typically conjures up images of wizards and goblins, but I use it here in a wider sense to describe simply *that which is not real*. So a fantasy environment could, for example, be a real location in which the element of fantasy is left to the players' imaginations, or it could be an immersive virtual world containing a host of mythical characters. It is the fantasy elements (the locations, characters, story and dialogue) that provide colour and background to a game.

Figure 2.1 The Vast Virtual World of *RuneScape* (image reproduced with permission of Jagex Ltd)

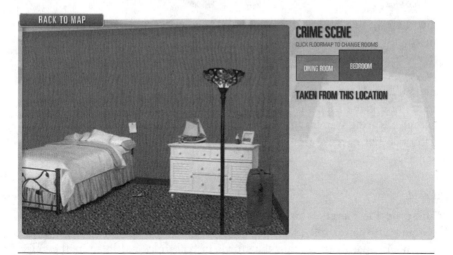

Figure 2.2 Detailed Exploration in *Sleuth* (image reproduced with permission of Hypothetical Software)

Goals

This characteristic refers to the provision of explicit aims and objectives. Goals let the players know what the purpose of a game is and why they are playing, as well as what they have to do to win or complete the game. Goals can be overarching and apply to the game as a whole (e.g. solve the mystery) or be smaller subgoals that need to be completed in order to achieve the overall aim of the game (e.g. unlock the door). Some games do not have predefined goals (e.g. children's make-believe games) and many simulation games are open-ended, but let the player play in a more flexible environment and define their own goals.

Interaction

This is the notion that players can influence the state of the game by taking action and, in turn, the game changes and provides feedback to the players, which they can use when deciding on their next action. Interaction can be simple, such as a quiz that provides feedback on answers given, or highly complex, such as a virtual world where players can interact with other players, game characters, objects and the environment itself. Crosswords are game-like activities where interaction does not take place, because the user changing the state of the game (i.e. adding a word to the crossword grid) does not lead to further changes on the grid itself, nor does it generate feedback from the environment.

Outcomes

These are related to, but distinct from, the goals of a game. They provide a mechanism for measuring the degree to which a goal has been achieved, how far a player is progressing towards a goal, or how one player is faring in comparison to others. For example, scoring is one way to demonstrate measurable outcomes, or the use of a progress bar can allow players to see how much of a game they have completed. Many simulation games have highly complex scoring systems that compare a whole range of variables, while other games do not have measurable outcomes but simply a win, lose or draw end state.

People

These are the players who take part in the game. In some games (such as online multi-player role-playing games) people play simultaneously; in some (e.g. many board games) they take turns in real time, and in some they play asynchronously over longer time periods (in cases such as online games with leader boards). Players play against each other competitively in many games, but can also collaborate with others to achieve group goals. Massively multi-player online role-playing games (MMORPGs) provide a good example of games that involves collaborative play where characters have to work together as a team to solve missions that cannot be completed by one player alone (although many of these games have a competitive angle also). Computer games are one area that has been traditionally dominated by single-player games, although it is common for players to play together in the same physical space, taking turns with an action game or working together to solve an adventure game. Recently, however, the increasing pervasiveness of networked computers and massive growth in online multi-player gaming has opened up the options available for games that involve collaboration with others.

Rules

These provide a set of instructions as to how the game should be played, and what constraints are in operation on the players. They can be both explicit (as in *the rules on the game box*) or implicit (such as codes of conduct within games). In the case of most computer games the rules are written into the design of the game, but there are usually various ways of cheating (e.g. using walkthroughs or hint forums). It is often the case that the rules of a certain genre are implicit, for example, in adventure games if you find a locked door you know that you are probably going to have to find a key. Therefore prior knowledge of that specific game genre is often useful in completing games of the same genre.

Safety

This is the idea that games are consequence-free environments that can be experimented in and that the outcomes of the game have no penalties or rewards in the real world. This characteristic is often not the case for people who play games at a professional level, for example, professional footballers, or games where there are other consequences outside of the game itself, such as gambling games. This may also be an unrealistic characteristic in education, where games may impact upon assessment grades, reputation or relationships.

You may have noticed one significant omission in this definition of games – where does *fun* come in? A difficulty that arises when devising a definition for games, or in trying to decide whether an activity can be classed as a game or not, is that the characteristics used to define a game are not all objective. For example, the degree of challenge and perceived safety may depend upon the circumstances and the particular individuals involved. However, on the whole, this framework uses objective characteristics so that the degree to which any given activity is like a game is inherent in the activity itself and not in an observer's perceptions of the activity (although clearly some characteristics may be open to the interpretation of the individual).

While including subjective elements within a definition may provide a more accurate understanding of reality, I feel it is not useful for trying to classify activities. For this reason, characteristics that are wholly subjective such as *fun*, *immersive* or *engaging* are not included in my definition of a game. For example, most people would agree that chess is a game, but if you include fun as a characteristic, how is the definition affected by the people (myself included) who don't find chess fun? Does it cease to be a game?

Activity: Reviewing Your Definition of a Game

Take five minutes to look back to the list of characteristics that you created to define a game in the previous activity.

- How many of your characteristics match mine?
- Do you have any characteristics that I don't have in my definition?
- Do you disagree with any of the characteristics I have defined? (If so, please go to the companion website and leave me some feedback to let me know what you think!)

What I have aimed to do by creating a definition based on characteristics is provide a framework for examining games, while making the notion of what makes an activity a game as open and inclusive as possible. This means that exciting learning activities (with many of the elements of games) do not get excluded on the grounds that they are *not* games, while still maintaining a focus for this book on the characteristics of games that make them exciting for learning. In the following subsection a number of activities that share characteristics with games, but are often considered not to be games, are discussed in relation to this framework.

Game-Like Activities

In this section I have identified five other activities that are similar to games in many ways and share a lot of their characteristics, but are often in the literature not considered to be games (this really depends on the perspective of the individual author). I will discuss these activities in relation to the framework of characteristics presented previously.

Simulations

A domain very closely associated with games is the use of simulations. There are many similarities between simulations and games, and the term *simulation-game* is often used to describe an activity that has characteristics of both (likewise some simulations are also games and some games are also simulations).

Simulations attempt to model an environment with a high degree of realism, and show genuine cause and effect and interaction between elements of the system being simulated. They can be explored and interrogated by the user, so providing an environment in which to experiment, but it is not necessary for a simulation to have explicit goals. Simulations are often used when there is some reason why the actual system cannot be experienced, such as cost, danger, inaccessibility or time (Rieber, 1996). Dormans (2008) argues that it is the role of a simulation to be a realistic representation, but this is not the function of games, which necessarily employ simplifications and enhancements to improve playability.

Virtual Worlds

There has been rapidly growing interest among educationalists in recent years regarding the potential for learning three-dimensional immersive virtual worlds such as *Second Life*. These worlds allow participants to interact with one another in a vast multi-user virtual space, where people create their own representations, or avatars, and can move around, interact with objects and locations, talk to other people and even create their own objects and environments. Virtual worlds are similar to games in that they look very much like gaming environments, they have massive worlds that can be explored, and often employ fantasy elements such as extraordinary locations or avatars with the ability to fly. They do not intrinsically have elements such as goals, outcomes, challenges or competition, although these factors are often built into areas of the virtual world to create mini in-world games.

Role Play

Another type of activity often associated with games are role plays, because of the use of fantasy and make-believe, and there is an obvious overlap in the area of role-playing games. Role play allows people to take part in a novel or imaginary experience by acting out the role of a character in a particular situation and experiencing empathy with that character to gain a better understanding of the situation from another perspective. Role-play situations often follow a set of rules and involve interaction with others, but do not always have defined goals (Feinstein *et al.*, 2002). While it is possible to have a role play that is a game (role-playing games themselves being a prime example), role play can have many other uses such as experiential learning, building empathy, therapy or relaxation.

Puzzles

Puzzles are another type of activity that shares many characteristics with games and, in fact, many games contain elements of puzzle-solving. Crawford

(1984) argues that it is the interaction that makes an activity a game rather than a puzzle, since puzzles do not actively respond to a player's moves. So, for example, a crossword could be classed as a puzzle rather than a game because it does not itself change as the player adds answers to the grid. Crawford also makes the point that 'we can easily turn many puzzles and athletic challenges into games and vice versa. For example, *Chess*, a game, has spawned a whole class of puzzles, the end-game problems' (Crawford, 1984, online).

Stories

Stories share the fantasy element with games; the creation of an imaginary world that can be explored (by the characters in the story within the limitations of the narrative, and vicariously by the reader) with characters and plot. Stories are essentially a linear narrative and non-interactive while games are typically non-linear and interactive, although there are exceptions to each of these definitions, a prime example being the genre of interactive fiction, which incorporates text-based adventure games. In the 1980s the first interactive storybooks appeared with popular series such as *Choose Your Own Adventure* blurring the boundaries between game-playing and storytelling. Rockler (1989) makes a convincing argument that mystery stories are in fact themselves games to some extent, particularly detective fiction, in that they have a set of rules (e.g. readers must be given access to all the clues, the suspects must be known and the murderer among them) and an outcome; however they do not offer the opportunity for the reader to interact with the story or affect the outcome.

Using the framework described in the previous section, all of the items described above – simulations, virtual worlds, role play, puzzles and stories – can be considered to be game-like to some degree because they share a number of characteristics with games. Although this is somewhat a semantic argument, I feel that adopting an inclusive definition of digital game-based learning enables us to move on from the (somewhat unhelpful) debate of whether an activity is or is not a game, to consider whether the game-like characteristics it possesses do, or do not, have potential for enhancing learning.

Hopefully after completing this activity with the games you selected earlier you will see that not all games exhibit all of the characteristics listed above (yet are still recognized as 'games' by many people). Use of the framework I have presented here is not an exact science (as you may have discovered when trying to apply it) but is really intended as a way of considering more deeply the elements that makes something a game, highlighting differences in types of gaming activities, and thinking about the characteristics of games that can influence the learning experience with them.

Activity: Application of the Definition

Using the list of five games you created in the first activity in this chapter, think about which of the characteristics of games mentioned in this chapter each activity possesses. Is the game competitive? Is there challenge? Is there an environment that can be explored? Is it set in a fantasy world? Is there interaction? Measurable outcomes? Is the game played with other people? Are there explicit rules? Does the game represent a safe environment?

Game Characteristics and Learning

From an educational perspective, there is a great deal of commonality between the characteristics of games and the characteristics of effective learning experiences. In my opinion, good learning activities are intrinsically challenging – but achievable – and stretch and engage the learners through gradually increasing levels of difficulty. The provision of explicit achievable goals is embedded in higher education practice through the provision of learning outcomes or objectives associated with each course (and often with smaller units of learning too). These objectives aim to be explicit, realistic and measurable so that learners are clear about what is expected of them and they can be formally assessed in an appropriate manner. This assessment can provide students with an indication of their progress, which is equivalent to an outcome (or result) in a game. The triangulation of learning objectives, activities and assessment, called constructive alignment (Biggs, 2003), is commonplace in the design of courses within higher education.

Interaction is also an essential component of learning, providing a mechanism for learners to identify misconceptions and test and modify their understandings. The provision of feedback is key, for without an identification of errors and areas for improvement it is difficult for individuals to expand their knowledge, improve their skills or see issues from different perspectives. Learning from other people through mentoring, discussion and group work is also an important part of learning in higher education. The potential for students to explore and investigate a subject to an appropriate level and depth for themselves is also, I feel, important for learning and for stimulating curiosity in the subject itself and from the questions that arise as further investigation is undertaken.

The presence of other people within the learning process is another key element, be they teachers, mentors, facilitators or other learners. I will argue in the next chapter that seeing games as fundamentally collaborative learning environments is an important step towards making full use of their potential for learning. While I would argue that other people are important, the relationship between players that is most appropriate for learning is less clear. Competition may act as a motivator for many students, but may also put unnecessary pressure on others, and from my own experience may act as a demotivational factor for some students who feel that they cannot compete (however, I do recognize that the implementation of any assessment system where marks or grades are comparative and made public will inevitably generate a competitive environment for students). Johnson and Johnson (1989) argue that cooperation is preferable to competition or the efforts of one person alone in many learning and work situation, but also highlight situations in which competition supports learning, such as when it is between groups rather than individuals. While competition is, for many, a key aspect of game play, it is one that needs to be applied with caution in an educational environment.

Two other characteristics of games that I feel also have to be applied with caution to learning are rules and safety. While rules can help guide and scaffold learners through learning activities, they can also stifle creativity in learning and should be seen as guidelines rather than hard-and-fast laws. While some rules, particularly those pertaining to conduct or appropriate behaviour, may be non-negotiable, others have the scope to be more flexible, enabling learners to take greater control over, and responsibility for, their own learning. Safety is another ambiguous area; while the idea of providing safe learning environments for students to test their assumptions and learn from their mistakes is sound, without some external motivation (e.g. assessment and degree classification) the degree to which students will realistically engage in learning is debatable.

The final characteristic, fantasy, is the one that has perhaps least obvious application to learning within higher education. However, imaginary and simulated scenarios and cases are commonly used in many aspects of higher education, business and medicine to name but two. In this context, the realism of the scenario is important as this will impact both on students' willingness to engage with it and on the transferability of learning to the real world. Taken as a whole, however, the characteristics of games discussed here relate to a great degree to the characteristics of good learning environments, although some have to be applied thoughtfully and with caution.

Chapter Summary

I presented ten characteristics that can be used to define a *game*. Not all games possess all of these characteristics, but the more an activity possesses the more essentially game-like I would consider it to be. This open definition aims to include a wide range of game-like activities that share characteristics with games.

The ten characteristics are: competition, challenge, exploration, fantasy, goals, interaction, outcomes, people, rules and safety.

Five other learning activities commonly associated with games – simulations, virtual worlds, role play, puzzles and stories – were also discussed in relation to this inclusive definition.

Finally, I discussed the relationship between each characteristic and effective learning. In my view challenge, goals, outcomes, interaction, exploration and people are fundamental to good learning, while rules, safety, competition and fantasy can affect the learning experience in a variety of ways.

Further Reading

K. Salen & E. Zimmerman (2004). *Rules of Play: Game Design Fundamentals*. Cambridge, MA: MIT Press. Chapter 7 of this comprehensive analysis of game design contains a comparative analysis of a host of different definitions from the literature on games.

N. Montfort (2005). *Twisty Little Passages: An Approach to Interactive Fiction*. Cambridge, MA: MIT Press. This provides a fascinating overview of the history and design of interactive fiction.

CHAPTER 3

Understanding the Pedagogy
of Digital Games

This chapter presents a pedagogic rationale for the use of digital games for learning in higher education, examining motivation, engagement and learning theory in relation to the use of computer games.

The aim of this chapter is to contextualize computer games within current pedagogic theory and provide a sound rationale for their use in higher education. I start by addressing the commonly made assumption that games are good for learning because students find them motivational, by looking at the differences between adult and children's motivations to learn in general, and to learn with games specifically. I discuss in particular the assumptions that are often made about games and motivation, and the acceptability of computer games for use with adult learners. This provides a rationale for why we have to think about the use of games with adults differently from their use with younger people. I next introduce a concept that I think is crucial when understanding the benefits of using games to learn – engagement – and explain why it is important for learning and why games can engender it.

The second half of the chapter examines several contemporary theories of learning and I will explain why, in my opinion, the true value of computer games is in conceiving them as active learning environments. By drawing on a range of theories of teaching and learning, I hope to present a compelling argument for the benefits of using computer games (certain games, in certain situations) to learn in the context of adult learners in higher education.

Learning and Motivation in Higher Education

The majority of the practice and research around the use of digital games in education has been undertaken with children, and often assumptions made from the use of games with children are applied wholesale to the use of computer games with adults. For example, I have lost count of the number of times I have heard people at conferences make statements like 'games are motivating' or 'all students like playing games to learn'. An understanding of how learners in higher education differ from school-age learners in their approaches to studying and motivations is important to appreciate the potential of digital games for learning in this sector.

Adult learning theory, or andragogy (Knowles, 1998), is a useful starting point for examining how the motivations of adults, with respect to learning, differ from those of children. Adult learning theory identifies ways in which the characteristics of adult learners, as related to their motivations and learning needs, differ from those of younger learners (although many of these points may also be true of some younger learners). The key premises of adult learning theory are shown below (Knowles, 1998):

- Adults need to *know why* they need to learn something before they are willing to invest time and energy in learning it. They will not necessarily be motivated to learn something simply because they are told to, so a clear purpose for a learning activity is essential.
- Adults need to be *in charge of their own learning* and to take increased responsibility for what, where, when and how they study, as well as understanding the process of learning itself. Learning needs to be increasingly learner-centred as students become more autonomous.
- Adults come from a *wide variety* of backgrounds and have different ranges of experience. Learning activities need to be designed to take into account, and exploit, this diversity.
- Adults become ready to learn when they need to *apply a skill or knowledge to the real world* to be able to cope effectively with real-life situations. Application of learning to the real world is paramount for motivation, and also aids retention of knowledge and skills.
- Adults are *task-focused* and learn things best in the context of using learning activities to achieve outcomes they want to accomplish.

Although many first-year undergraduates come straight from school, and have much in common with younger school-based learners in terms of their motivations to learn, they have made a choice to learn at university and, in many cases, in the UK anyway, will be paying for the experience. This naturally changes the way in which many students approach study and the expectations they have from the university experience. As students progress through their university careers they are likely to adopt more and more of the characteristics of adult learners described above. Development of learner autonomy is a key issue for institutions, as many students are not as autonomous as institutions or employers would wish, possibly owing to the assessment-focused school system, which in my opinion does not prepare many students for the demands of university; and in part to students increasingly being seen as customers, with parents becoming more involved and influential in their children's education, reducing the need for students to take responsibility for themselves.

In recent years there has also been increasing diversity in the student population, with a growing representation of mature learners in higher education, typically defined as individuals 'who have returned to learning after some kind of separation from a formal educational environment such as school, college or university' (Hodson *et al.*, 2001: 327). These individuals may typically have more work and personal responsibilities, caring commitments, greater life experiences and a need for greater study guidance. However, increased pressure of life and work commitments and limited time to devote to study (particularly because of the need to earn money during the time spent at university) is becoming ever more true of traditional students also.

The ways in which students in higher education approach study are clearly different from how children learn; motivation and purpose are paramount. This then calls into question the acceptability of digital games for learning with adults, many of whom may perceive games in the context of learning as frivolous or a waste of time, who may not find them motivating or play games at all in their leisure time.

Activity: Reflecting on Your Own Motivations

Take ten minutes to answer the following questions.

If you play computer games, by choice, in your leisure time, write down three (or more) reasons for playing.

If you don't play computer games, select another activity that you choose to participate in during your leisure time, and write down three (or more) reasons for undertaking that activity.

Consider whether you personally would find a game to be a motivational way to learn. If not, why not? What aspects do you find demotivational?

It is important to recognize that not everyone is interested in playing computer games at all, and there may be a variety of different motivations for those who do play – not all compatible with learning. In order to examine the attitudes of adult learners towards learning with games, I carried out a small study to look at the acceptability of games for learning and whether they were perceived as motivational. In the sections that follow I discuss the findings of this study and their implications for the use of digital games with learners in higher education.

A Study on Adult Attitudes to Games

When I originally began studying games for learning I made the mistake of assuming that games are intrinsically motivational, for most students anyway (initially it never occurred to me that there is another way to perceive games because I am a keen games player and personally find them motivational). This is also a common assumption in the literature and one that I did not think to question. During an initial series of focus groups, however, I was surprised to discover that several of the participants did not play games at all, were not in the least motivated to use them to learn and were even doubtful that they were at all appropriate in a university setting. This led to a change in direction of my interests to investigate the assumptions made about games and motivation in adults, and whether they are even an acceptable learning medium at all in this context.

In order to investigate student perceptions of games, I carried out a small-scale mixed-methods study consisting of in-depth interviews and use of a questionnaire with a larger population (Whitton, 2007). These interviews ($n = 12$) aimed to gain an insight into the different perceptions of students who were – and were not – naturally disposed to play games recreationally, examined their motivations for playing games (and other recreational activities) and their attitudes towards game-based learning in education. These interviews were followed up with a student survey ($n = 200$) that aimed to generate a larger picture of student motivational preferences regarding games. In the three subsections that follow I will discuss the results of this research in relation to student motivations to play games in their leisure time, the relationship to playing games for learning and the overall acceptability of games for learning in the context of higher education.

Motivations to Play Games

From the interviews carried out as part of this study, it was clear, and perhaps unsurprising, that the participants who considered themselves to be game players had different motivations for playing games than those who did not play games by choice in their leisure time. Among the game players, there were three primary motivations for playing games:

• *Mental stimulation*, a motivation to play predominantly for the intellectual challenge. Players may prefer to solve puzzles, problem-solving games and other types of game that are mentally challenging.

- *Social interaction*, a motivation to play with other people and to interact with other people, either in competition, collaboration or simply in the same social gaming space. People with this primary motivation may prefer multi-user games and team games.
- *Physical challenge*, a motivation to play to achieve physical goals, which could include exercise, physical exertion, as well as computer games that involve dexterity or hand–eye coordination.

Compared to those people interviewed who played games by choice in their leisure time, the non-game-players were found to have very different motivations. Although these people did not consider themselves to be game players, they did occasionally play games, under two particular circumstances: to alleviate boredom, usually for short periods of time, and to facilitate social situations, perhaps in an awkward gathering or as a way of getting to know people. In both of these situations the game was seen as a means to achieving another end (i.e. passing time or making a social occasion easier) rather than being motivational for itself.

As well as identifying a range of different motivations for playing games, I feel it is important to recognize from this (admittedly small) study that a range of different motivations for playing exist, and it is an oversimplification to assume that any game is motivational simply because it is a game. Different people are motivated by different types of game, and not all types are necessarily suitable in the context of higher education. Even if learners consider themselves to be *game players* in general, the motivational potential of a particular game will depend upon the individuals concerned and the type of game used.

Motivation to Learn with Games

In addition to exploring why people play games in leisure time, I was also keen to examine whether they found the use of games to be a motivational way to learn, and if there was any link between wanting to play games as a recreational activity and wanting to learn with them. I carried out research with 200 undergraduate and postgraduate computing students. This group were used for two reasons: first, the pragmatic reason that this was a large group of students that could be easily accessed as I was working with the School of Computing at the time; and second, I hypothesized that computing students (predominantly male, under 25, computer-literate) would be a population of students in higher education likely to engage with games in their leisure time. I recognize that while findings from this group can't be generalized to other groups of students, it is a group where engagement with games might be expected to be higher than average. I was interested to see – even in a group that might be expected to be motivated to use games for learning – the actual level of student motivation to use games; this turned out to be far lower than the rhetoric might have us believe.

In terms of recreational gaming, 87 per cent of the sample played computer games in their leisure time, providing evidence that this is a group who are motivated by games, for entertainment at least. In terms of being motivated to learn from games, however, only just under two-thirds of the group (63 per cent) responded that they would find games positively motivating, 28 per cent that they would not be motivated either way and 9 per cent said that they would actually find using games to learn demotivational. While this is a positive result in one way, in that it provides evidence that games are motivational for many students, what I find more interesting is that over a third of this group said that they would not be positively motivated by using a game to learn. There could be a number of reasons for this, including a lack of understanding of what an educational game entails, prior negative experiences with educational games (although there was no link between previous experience with educational games and motivation), a wish to create a boundary between leisure and work, or a feeling that games are *frivolous* and inappropriate for education.

In order to test the assumption that those people who are motivated to play games in their leisure time will also be motivated to use them to learn, I carried out a statistical analysis to see if there was any link between motivation to play games recreationally and motivation to play games to learn. A chi-squared test was used to examine whether students who were motivated to play computer games in their leisure time were more likely to also be motivated to learn with games. There was no evidence that there is any relationship between a motivation to play computer games for leisure and a motivation to use them for learning (a detailed description of the statistical analysis undertaken is available in Whitton, 2007).

The Acceptability of Games for Learning

The research described in the previous two sections indicates that the use of computer games for learning may not be as motivational for students as is sometimes assumed. I was also interested, however, in whether games would even be seen as acceptable in the context of higher education, and there is some evidence that this is the case.

The in-depth interviews also aimed to provide some justification for the acceptability of game-based learning. The perceptions of game-based learning were, perhaps surprisingly (given that half of the sample did not play games in their leisure time), positive. Every single person interviewed said that they were open to consider the idea of a game to learn – but *only if they felt that it was the most effective way to learn something* and not simply being used as a way to increase motivation (several interviewees pointed out that they would consider *any* method of teaching and learning if it was the most effective way to learn something).

What I feel is important to take from this is that educational games for students in higher education need to be thoughtfully designed, with sound pedagogic principles at their heart, have very specific and clearly communicated learning outcomes, and obvious benefits over other methods of learning. The key point from this research is, for me, that the reason for using computer games in teaching and learning should not be simply that they are assumed to be motivational; this is not in itself a sufficient rationale for using a game in education – particularly not in higher education. The rationale for using games must be that they can embody sound educational principles and are an effective way to learn in the context in which they are used. It is crucial also that students are aware of the educational benefits of any game and feel that it has a true purpose in the context of their studies. If a game is perceived by the students as being a valuable way to learn then it is likely that they will be motivated to use it to enhance their learning experience, not simply because it is a game.

I would argue therefore that the real value of games lies, not in their motivational benefits, but in the sound educational principles that many embody and their ability to engage students (because they can be good learning experiences). In the next section I consider the importance of engagement for learning, and the ways that games can be used to engender engagement and create effective learning experiences.

Digital Games and Engagement

I think that one of the important features of digital games in the context of learning is their ability to create engagement for the user. The term 'engagement' is not one commonly used in the games industry (which tend to focus on 'fun' and 'entertainment') but I think is of particular relevance when considering educational games. There are many different definitions of exactly what is meant by engagement but I particularly like the one provided by Benyon and colleagues (2005: 61):

> engagement is concerned with all the qualities of an experience that really pull people in – whether this is a sense of immersion that one feels when reading a good book, or a challenge one feels when playing a good game, or the fascinating unfolding of a radio drama.

Benyon and colleagues also identify a number of key elements that contribute to engagement in virtual environments, including a sense of authenticity and identification with the environment, the ability of the environment to adapt to the needs of the user, a compelling narrative, immersion and flow (Benyon *et al.*, 2005, based on Shedroff, 2001). I find flow theory (Csikszentmihalyi, 2002) a particularly useful way of understanding and defining the notion of engagement. Being in the state of flow is being in a state of *optimal experience*, and is described as 'the state in which people are so involved in an activity that nothing else seems to matter; the experience itself is so enjoyable that people will do it even at great cost, for the sheer sake of doing it' (Csikszentmihalyi, 2002: 4). In my view, being in a state of *flow* is very similar to being highly engaged.

Flow theory states that the following elements add to enjoyment, some being intrinsic in an activity itself and some being related to the state of mind of the participant. The more of these elements that are present, the more enjoyable, engaging and immersive an activity is:

- a challenge that requires skills with an attainable goal and known rules;
- complete absorption in the activity;
- clear goals;
- immediate feedback;
- concentration on the task in hand;
- a sense of control, lacking the sense of worry about losing control;
- loss of self-consciousness;
- transformation of time.

However, flow theory is not without its critics. Draper (1999) expands the theory further, arguing that flow is not a single concept but is actually broken down into u-flow and c-flow (where u-flow is a smooth but unconsciously managed flow of actions such as occur when driving a car, whereas c-flow requires the total conscious attention). He also hypothesizes that flow only occurs where there is a deep connection between the activity and the participant's core values and aspirations. Salen and Zimmerman (2004) argue that flow is not intrinsic to a game but is dependent on the state of mind of the player and the interactions with the game.

A second theory that I find useful when understanding engagement emerged from the work of Malone (1980), who produced some of the seminal research in gaming and engagement. He investigated the characteristics that make digital games engaging and considered how those features that make games captivating might be used to make game-based learning more interesting and enjoyable. Malone initially presented three aspects of games that he argues lead to increased engagement: challenge, fantasy and curiosity.

Appropriate *challenge* can be created by the use of goals, which should be obvious, compelling and adaptable, coupled with an uncertainty by the player of whether these goals can be met. Short-term goals are more motivating than long-term and fixed goals (e.g. winning a game) are more motivating than emergent goals (e.g. painting a picture). Creating the optimal level of challenge for an individual is seen as key, where a goal is seen as attainable but requires effort to achieve.

Fantasy is the notion of a storyline or imaginary scenario in which a game is situated, and can be intrinsic to learning (where the skill or knowledge to be learned is closely related to the fantasy, for example in a detective game where the player has to carry out a chemical analysis to process evidence relating to the crime), or extrinsic (where the skill does not depend on the fantasy, such as a quiz game set in space where answering questions correctly is rewarded by sections of game play). Malone argues that intrinsic fantasies are generally more interesting and purposeful in an educational context.

Curiosity, according to Malone, takes two forms: sensory and cognitive. Sensory curiosity involves the use of light, sound or other sensory stimuli, and cognitive curiosity involves completing an individual's mental map of the world and ensuring that understanding is comprehensive and consistent. Curiosity can be stimulated where actions taken in a game lead to feedback that is both surprising and constructive.

Malone and Lepper (1987) extend Malone's original theory to include an additional factor: control over the (learning) environment. *Control* is considered as three separate areas: contingency (where interactions within the game and the interface are logical); choice (where a large number of options are available); and power (where a decision is perceived to be influential on the effect).

Although I earlier refer to Malone's work as *seminal*, I think it is worth making a couple of points regarding the value of this work as related to learning in higher education today. First, this research was conducted with children, and although Malone's findings may be replicable with adults, there is limited evidence of this, and while some of the factors intuitively make sense when applied to adult engagement (e.g. challenge) other factors are less compelling (e.g. fantasy). Secondly, Malone's work took place during the early 1980s, a period when computer games were new to most children and were to some extent engaging purely for their novelty value; today, games are ubiquitous and people are far more sophisticated in their expectations. Even so, Malone's work is still regularly used as a basis for work on game design and engagement and has been endorsed and applied by many other researchers since its inception. Overall, I tend to take the view that much is still valid and applicable to students in higher education, but it should still be applied with some caution.

Activity: Understanding What Engages You

Can you think of the last time you were so immersed in an activity that you realized that time simply seemed to have flown by? Can you think of another activity that you've undertaken recently where time seemed to go on forever?

Take five minutes to write down the differences between these two experiences that contributed to engagement (or lack of it).

For each activity did you find it challenging? Did you feel that you had control over it? Were you curious to find out what was happening? Was there an element of losing yourself in a fantasy?

Different people will find different activities engaging to different degrees at different times. Being able to recognize what factors contribute to greater engagement for yourself will help in the design of engaging learning experience for others.

In the previous chapter, I talked about *fun* as a potential characteristic for defining games. I think it is also worth briefly mentioning fun here in relation to engagement. In the context of games, I believe that fun can be a component of an engaging experience, but not an essential one. For example, I remember being highly engaged several years ago the first time I watched the film *Schindler's List*, but it is not an experience I would ever describe as fun. In relation to games for learning, I feel that while fun might be a nice by-product, it is the development of learner engagement that is important for creating effective learning experiences.

In the section that follows, I explore some of the contemporary theories of learning and teaching that I feel provide a strong rationale for the use of computer games in higher education.

A Rationale for Digital Games in Higher Education

In this section, I examine some of the pedagogic theories that I think relate to the use of computer games in learning, and provide my reasons for advocating their use. When I discuss computer games here, I do so with the caveat that I am only really talking about certain types of game that I think are most appropriate for use in higher education – this is covered in more detail in the following chapter. This section looks at four particular educational theories and considers how they fit in with the ideas of digital game-based learning in higher education.

I acknowledge that games have a place in teaching facts and knowledge, may be useful for providing a context for repetition and recall (particularly in areas where memorization is important such as language learning), and can be used effectively for training and skills development. However, the area where I feel that they have the greatest potential in higher education is in the development and application of high-level transferable skills – such as analysis, critical evaluation, autonomy, and team working – situated within specific areas. It is in this context that I examine four areas of learning theory in the sections that follow. I will discuss active learning and constructivism, experiential learning, collaborative learning, and problem-based learning and highlight the importance of these theoretical constructs in relation to providing a pedagogic rationale for the use of computer games in learning.

The way in which teaching and learning has been perceived has changed significantly over the last century. Behaviourism had long been the dominant school of thought, but cognitivism because popular in the late 1950s, and then became the customary way of conceptualizing learning. More recently the constructivist paradigm has become the prevailing way in which the theory of learning is described (Cooper, 1993). Behaviourists saw the mind as a *black box* that can be studied by observing behaviour, where knowledge can be transferred directly to a student by listening to an expert, and learning can be *drilled* and reinforced; in essence the mind was a vessel to be filled with knowledge. Cognitivist thinkers focused on the thought processes behind behaviours, and aimed to understand the ways in which the mind works, looking particularly at cognition, sensory systems, brain processes and memory. The constructivist perspective builds on some of the understanding of the workings of the mind developed through cognitivism but holds the view that, rather than there being a single truth that exists in the world, personal understandings of a phenomenon are constructed by individuals through experience, discussion and application. The theories that are discussed in the remainder of this chapter are influenced by the constructivist perspective; it is this way of conceptualizing the learning process that has greatly influenced my own thinking regarding computer games and their potential for learning.

Constructivism and Active Learning

Constructivism is not a single theory but a number of related theories and perspectives associated with ideas of active learning. Bruner (1966) first proposed the idea that learning is an active process (rather than the passive transmission of knowledge advocated by behaviourists) and that learners construct their own understandings of a subject by engaging in activities and building on past knowledge and experience. I find the principles of constructivism provided by Savery and Duffy (1995) particularly useful as a way of summarizing what is actually a highly complex range of interwoven theoretical constructs. They say that there are three fundamental precepts:

- *Situated cognition.* The idea that individuals' understandings are developed by interactions with their environments; they are formed by a combination of content, context, activity and goal and are individually constructed; they cannot be shared, but compatibility of understandings can be tested through discussion with others.

- *Cognitive puzzlement.* Cognitive conflict – or puzzlement – is the stimulus for learning and determines the organization and nature of what is learned; there is always a goal for learning something and this goal is a primary factor in determining what the learner attends to and what is constructed.
- *Social collaboration.* Knowledge evolves through social negotiation and by testing the viability of individual understandings on others; the social environment is critical to the development of understanding, and other individuals are a primary mechanism for providing sources of alternative views to challenge thinking.

Fundamental to the constructivist perspective is the idea that people learn by constructing their own conceptions about the world by problem-solving and personal discovery. The design of student-centred online learning environments has been very much influenced by the constructivist perspective (e.g. Grabinger *et al.*, 1997; Land & Hannafin, 2000). I take the view that certain types of computer game can be viewed as constructivist learning environments, where they are defined as:

> a place where learners may work together and support each other as they use a variety of tools and information resources in their guided pursuit of learning goals and problem-solving activities.
>
> (Wilson, 1996: 5)

This definition clearly includes many types of collaborative computer game. Honebein (1996) presents seven pedagogic goals of the design of constructivist learning environments. They should support students to take responsibility for what and how they learn, expose learners to multiple points of view, encourage students to take ownership of the learning process, make learning authentic and relevant, be based on real-life activities, support social learning, use multiple modes of representation and rich media.

These goals of constructivist learning environments are particularly relevant to learning with digital games in higher education; their principles are embodied in certain types of computer game and I would argue, therefore, that certain types of game (I'll come to which ones in the next chapter) are in fact constructivist learning environments. For example, role-playing games can provide the opportunity for learners to explore and navigate immersive virtual worlds using rich media, simulations can create authentic contexts for rehearsing skills that can be transferred to the real world, and adventure games can present a forum and context for problem-solving. Collaboration, learning with others and exploring multiple perspectives are fundamental to the constructivist perspective, and multi-user games or collaborative game-playing in the same physical space are just two ways that games can be used to foster social interaction and collaboration.

However, proving support for students taking responsibility for planning and structuring their learning, and gaining understanding of and engagement in the learning process are not goals that are often explicitly designed or considered in computer games. It is therefore crucial to consider the context in which games for learning are used, their role in the curriculum and the activities that precede and follow any game for learning. Prensky makes the argument that if games are used for learning then 'learning would happen almost without the learners' realizing it, in pursuit of beating the game' (2001: 24). Without an understanding of the learning process and structured reflection, to support learners to understand the process, context and transferability of learning, I would argue that the value of learning undertaken in this way is questionable – particularly in the context of higher education.

The notion of situated cognition and provision of context for learning is one that is particularly supported by computer games. For example, in *Sherlock Holmes and the Case of the Silver Earring* (see Figure 3.1) players have to undertake a variety of experiments to analyse evidence found while investigating a crime.

Figure 3.1 Experimenting in *Sherlock Holmes and the Case of the Silver Earring* (image reproduced with permission of DreamCatcher Interactive Inc.)

Outside the wider context of the game, these experiments and chemical analyses would seem pointless and mundane, but the game helps to provide purpose and context for the activity.

Experiential Learning

The constructivist perspective also holds the idea that students learn better by undertaking an active role in the learning process, by exploring and experiencing authentic contexts for themselves and discovering their own meanings from the experience. The Experiential Learning Cycle (Kolb, 1984) presents a model that emphasizes the importance of active learning, including planning, reflection and gaining theoretical underpinning. According to this cycle, learning takes place as part of a sequence of steps where a learner starts by actively taking part in a learning activity that provides a concrete experience; this is followed by personal reflection on the experience. This reflection is then followed by the application of known theories to the experience, or the derivation of rules from it; and finally the learning is used to inform, modify and plan the next learning activity.

One of the benefits of digital games, and in fact of many forms of technology-enhanced learning, is the ability of a computer to provide the interaction and feedback that is crucial to the experiential learning cycle and to the whole learning process. Computer games have the ability to facilitate a whole range of types of interaction from simple items that can be clicked and movement through a linear sequence to highly complex interactive virtual worlds. Salen and Zimmerman (2004) give examples for four modes of interactivity that occur in games (they also refer to them as levels of engagement). These are described as cognitive interactivity, the psychological, emotional and intellectual participation in the game; functional interactivity, the actual controls that the player uses to interact with the game; explicit interactivity whereby the player makes choices and responds to events in the game; and beyond-the-object interactivity, which relates to interaction outwith the single experience of the game. This feedback cycle is essential to the process of learning and the fact that a game can make this implicit within the virtual gaming world, situating feedback seamlessly within the game, makes it an incredibly powerful learning tool. Feedback is an essential part of interaction, and Oxland (2004) describes several different types of feedback that computer games can facilitate, which he describes as visual, audio, action (where explicit feedback is proved after a player's action has occurred), NPC (from Non-Player-controlled Characters), accumulative (so that feedback provides an indication of relative progression through the game), emotional, fulfilment (the feeling of achievement from having solved a puzzle) and informative.

Gee (2003) argues that computer games reflect the experiential learning cycle because students must examine the virtual environment of the game, reflect on the situation and form a hypothesis about what is happening, take action and then investigate the virtual world to see what effect their action had. I take the view that this cycle may map on to learning within the game world itself, but does not necessarily provide students with scope for the meta-cognitive processes required for them to be able to transfer the learning outside of the context of the game into the real world. I feel that it is important to recognize that game-based learning within the context of higher level skills in higher education is necessarily part of a larger learning process and needs to be surrounded with other activities to foster and support reflection and the experiential learning cycle as a whole. Computer games for learning should be considered in relation to the other activities and reflection that surround them and not simply as stand-alone activities.

Computer games have the advantage that they can situate experience within a meaningful context. For example, the *Crime Scene Investigation* series of games are good examples of detective games that have the potential to support learning. The player has to collect and analyse evidence and witness statements in order to solve crimes. To complete the games players have to use their powers of observation, apply a range of forensic techniques and think critically about the evidence presented. Even in the case of games designed for entertainment, where real-life procedures may be truncated or altered to increase the game playability, there is still potential for using the game as a discussion point for how the game world differs from reality.

Collaborative Learning

Also related to the constructivist notion of learning is the idea of social constructivism and collaborative learning that highlights the importance of students working together, sharing and clarifying ideas and opinions, developing communication skills and learning from one another. Working collaboratively enables students to work to their strengths, develop critical thinking skills and creativity, validate their ideas and appreciate a range of individual learning styles, skills, preferences and perspectives (McConnell, 2000; Palloff & Pratt, 2003).

Vygotsky (1978), one of the seminal authors in the field of social constructivism is particularly concerned with the collaborative aspects of learning. He proposed that learning takes place at a social level first and then at an individual level; his theory of Zones of Proximal Development contends that such a zone is the difference between what a student can learn working alone, and what he or she can achieve when being supported and guided by a teacher or some other expert. Participating in communities of practice provides a legitimate and ongoing way of learning from others as part of a group, through apprenticeship and education in the context of the group norms, processes and identity (Lave & Wenger, 1991).

A major advantage of the growth and ubiquity of networked computing is the potential to develop virtual communities of learners and virtual communities of gamers. Collaborative online learning allows students from across the world to come together in a virtual space – synchronously or asynchronously – and work together on task or discuss issues and share viewpoints, 'sharing resources, knowledge, experience and responsibility through reciprocal collaborative learning' (McConnell, 2006: 11). Multi-user gaming communities provide a similar platform for collaboration and the ability to learn with others. Studies of leisure users of massively multi-player online role-playing games (MMORPGs) have found evidence of collaborative learning, development of communities of practice (Steinkuehler, 2004) as well as the potential for learning a range of group skills, including the etiquette of meeting people, group management, cooperation and social interaction (Ducheneaut & Moore, 2005). However, it is not just computer games that are designed to be multi-user that have the potential for collaboration; by framing game-based activities with briefing and reflective activities there is scope for collaboration at all stages of the learning process.

Problem-Based Learning

The problem-based learning (and the closely associated enquiry-based learning) approach to learning and teaching has clear parallels with the activities that take place in certain types of computer game, such as puzzle or adventure games. Problem-based learning is a methodology that involves small groups of students working together to tackle real-life, cross-disciplinary problems. The teacher assumes the role of facilitator rather than subject expert. Resources are made available to the students but information on how to tackle the problem itself is not provided, and work is carried out intensively on one problem at a time. This provides activity-based learning, with students taking more responsibility for their own learning, and learning in a real-world context (Boud & Feletti, 1991). Enquiry-based learning is similar to problem-based learning where learning is based around a scenario and students formulate their own questions and issues. The internet is also often central to facilitating problem- or enquiry-based learning as it allows students to research topics to a level and depth that is appropriate for them.

Researchers have highlighted that computer games have the facility to create real-life problem-solving experiences. Kiili (2005: 17) argues that 'games provide a meaningful framework for offering problems to students. In fact, a game itself is a big problem that is composed of smaller causally linked problems.' In a survey of 25 educational experts using game-based learning, de Freitas found

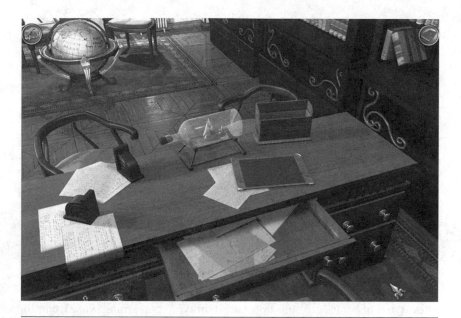

Figure 3.2 *And Then There Were None*; An Adventure Game Based on the Agatha Christie Novel (image reproduced with permission of DreamCatcher Interactive Inc.)

that in general those interviewed advocated the use of simulations and games for problem-based learning (de Freitas, 2006). The presentation of problems to be solved is fundamental to many different types of computer game and, I would argue, is fundamental to creating purposeful learning that can be applied to other contexts.

Many types of games, but particularly adventure games, present problem-solving environments in which players have to engage with the story, characters and problems presented in order to complete the game. For example, in the adventure game based on the Agatha Christie novel, *And Then There Were None* (see Figure 3.2), players have to explore an island, talk to characters and solve a series of puzzles in order to resolve the problems around which the game is based.

Even when the context of the game is not directly relevant to the subject area, the transferable skills associated with problem-solving, such as lateral thinking, information gathering and analysis, and developing and testing solutions can be valuable nonetheless.

Activity: Considering Pedagogic Approaches in Games

For this activity I'm going to refer to the three games that I presented in the Introduction to the book (if you haven't played them yet, now would be a good time).

For each of these three games, consider:

- What might someone learn from playing the game?
- Does the game support learning through doing or through telling?
- Do players have to work with others to achieve their goals?
- Are problems presented that players have to solve?

The three games that I provided as examples have been designed primarily for entertainment rather than for learning, so you might initially find it difficult to see any educational value in them (and I am certainly not advocating that these are excellent examples of games for learning). However, I believe that these types of games can still support certain types of learning. *RuneScape*, for example, supports players in working together strategically to solve quests, *NotPron* requires players to think laterally and work out technical puzzles, while *Sleuth* requires logical deduction in order to solve the 'crimes' presented.

While I accept that there are other learning paradigms and that games-based learning has been used successfully in an instructional, drill-and-practice and skills-based manner in higher and adult education, the focus of this book is unashamedly on the conception of computer games as active learning environments in which students can learn by doing, by undertaking purposeful and meaningful tasks, reflect on their experiences and work with others to achieve their learning goals.

I believe that understanding the sound pedagogic principles that are embedded within many digital games can not only help us understand how games for learning can be better designed and implemented, but can also enhance the way that all learning and teaching takes place in our higher education institutions. In the following chapter I discuss the range of different types of games that are available to educators and examine the different types of learning that can be undertaken with these games.

Chapter Summary

The chapter started by discussing the differences between adult learning and children's learning, highlighting the fact that adults: (a) need a clear motivation for learning; (b) need to be self-directing and self-reflective; (c) have a variety of prior experience; (d) become ready to learn something when they need to apply it; and (e) are task-orientated in their learning.

The second section, on adults' motivations to play games and engagement, presented evidence that adults play games for mental stimulation, social interaction, physical challenge, time-wasting and group facilitation. It highlighted that it is important that all motivations are considered and that a desire to play games recreationally does not necessarily relate to a desire to use games to learn. While computer games may be motivational for some it is likely that they will only be acceptable to all if they are designed with sound pedagogic principles in mind and are perceived by students as an effective method of learning. I also highlighted that the concept of engagement is an important factor when considering learning from digital games.

Four theories of teaching and learning that particularly relate to the use of computer games were also discussed. The concepts of active learning and constructivism, experiential learning, collaborative learning and problem-based learning all provide a theoretical pedagogic rationale for the use of computer games in higher education.

Further Reading

S. M. Alessi & S. R. Trollip (2001). *Multimedia for Learning*. Boston, MA: Allyn & Bacon. Although not explicitly linked to games, Chapter 2 provides an excellent critical overview of many of the theories discussed in this chapter.

K. Oxland (2004). *Gameplay and Design*. Harlow: Addison-Wesley. Design of interaction in games and feedback can be found in Chapter 6, 'Feedback and Fulfilment'.

CHAPTER 4

Identifying Types of Digital Games for Learning

This chapter identifies the different types of digital game available, discusses those that are most appropriate for different types of learning in higher education, and presents two emerging areas in educational gaming.

I first present a range of different genres of computer game and consider the appropriateness of each for learning in higher education. Secondly, I approach the issues of types of game for learning from a different angle and consider the different types of learning that take place, and the potential uses of games in these contexts. The third part of the chapter looks at two of the areas in which I feel there is a great emerging potential for the use of digital games for learning – alternate reality games and mobile gaming.

Types of Digital Game Available to Educators

When you think about the term digital games for learning, you probably already have some notion or mental picture of a particular type of game in mind, possibly based on previous experiences with games used for entertainment as well as learning. In this section I aim to provide an overview of the main types of digital game, without dwelling too much on providing a complete taxonomy, but trying to build a picture of the types of game that exist, in order to consider the potential of different types for learning in higher education.

My own background is primarily in the use of games that are played on a multi-purpose computer (such as a laptop or desktop machine), rather than those that are specifically designed for consoles or other gaming machines, and to some extent that is reflected in the genres presented here. I tend to favour general-purpose machines as platforms for games for higher education. Many students already have their own computer, or can at least access one through their institution, making them more accessible than dedicated gaming machines. In addition, the range of games available is, I feel, generally more appropriate for learning, and developing games for generic machines is more feasible for the majority of those working in academia.

Many researchers have tried to categorize computer games into types or taxonomies, and although there are often large differences between them, there is also much similarity in terms of the general classifications. There is no single definitive agreement of what genres of computer game exist and Oxland (2004: 24) makes the point that:

> identifying what constitutes a genre has been fraught with ambiguity, mainly due to the creative flux our industry introduced, the overlap of genres and the constant churn of technology and ideas.

What I am not trying to do in this section is provide a comprehensive taxonomy of all the game genres that exist, but instead I have selected seven distinct genres to discuss in order to put forward the idea that different types of game exist and each has different benefits and drawbacks in terms of their applicability for learning in Higher Education. I feel that these seven classifications provide enough distinctions to provide an idea of the types of different game that are available, without being overwhelming. As mentioned previously, there is a lot of overlap between genres of game and individual games may fall into several categories; there will also be games that do not fit into the typical description of the genre given here. However, what I aim to do with the following list is provide a feel for the types of game that are available, consider how they might be classified, and what use they may be in the context of learning.

Adventure

Adventure games are one of the oldest forms of computer game, going back to the early text adventures and interactive fiction of the 1970s and 1980s. They involve the player undertaking series of tasks or puzzles in which they must interact with the virtual world, performing actions, talking to characters and manipulating objects in order to achieve the objectives of the game, often to solve some mystery or complete a quest. There is also usually a compelling narrative that holds the plot together, such as in the popular game *The Longest Journey* (see Figure 4.1 below) that uses rich graphics in futuristic and fantasy locations to provide an engaging backdrop to the puzzles and stories that need to be solved.

Although the original adventure games were text-based, contemporary commercial adventure games tend use graphics, offering three-dimensional worlds that players can navigate. There is also a growing popularity of simpler web-based adventures, known as point-and-click games, which typically provide two-dimensional environments in which the player has to navigate through rooms and make objects interact to solve the puzzles presented (see Figure 4.2).

Adventure games generally depend on mental agility rather than physical dexterity and tend not to be time-dependent. Some adventures combine elements of both and it is common for adventure games to contain mini-games in another genre (for example the puzzle embedded in the Nancy Drew adventure game in Figure 4.3). In terms of education, adventure games can present a context for problem-solving and lateral thinking, where players have to work out the appropriate actions in order to achieve a goal.

Platform

Platform games involve the movement of the player character through a landscape (usually two-dimensional), jumping up and down between platforms, avoiding obstacles and enemies, and picking up treasure, usually with some

Figure 4.1 *The Longest Journey* Provides a Rich Interactive Narrative (image reproduced with permission of Funcom)

Figure 4.2 *The Bonte Room*, a Popular Point-and-Click Adventure Game (image reproduced with permission of Bart Bonte)

overall goal in mind and often in the context of a narrative. Platform games require physical dexterity and the aim is usually to score points and complete levels. The types of skills that they develop are hand–eye coordination, planning and strategizing, problem-solving (the sequence of steps required to get over a particular obstacle for instance) and the ability to think quickly.

Puzzle

Puzzle games primarily involve problem-solving (unsurprisingly), can take many forms – including words, logic, mathematics – and are often based on traditional puzzles (for example online crosswords or spot-the-difference). Simple puzzle games can be stand-alone but they are also often embedded within a larger narrative structure so that solving the puzzles will complete some larger quest or story. It is common for puzzles to be embedded within

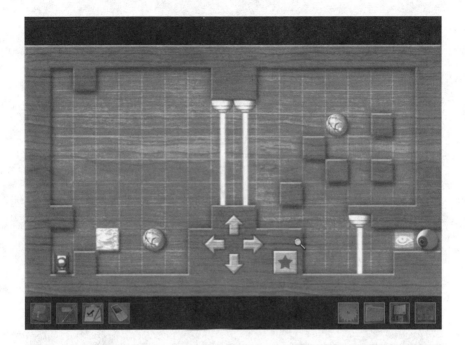

Figure 4.3 A Mini-game Within *Nancy Drew and the Crystal Skull* (image reproduced with permission of Bart Bonte)

other genres such as adventure games as mini-games. Puzzles can be used to support a variety of different types of learning depending on the type of puzzle, including logic, spatial awareness, verbal skills, numeracy skills, and spelling (see, for example, the Bookworm game in Figure 4.4). I would also include quizzes in this category, and they are an example of a game activity that can be used in almost any area of a curriculum, but primarily for recall of facts.

Role Play

Role play games emerged from the face-to-face role-playing games and involve the player taking on the role of a character in another (usually fantasy-based) world (see, for example, *Guild Wars* in Figure 4.5). The player can undertake a range of activities including solving quests, fighting, treasure hunting, and interacting with other characters (either other players in the game world or non-player characters). There is usually a mix of problem-solving skills required as well as strategy and sometimes physical dexterity, and although single-player role-playing games exist, they are commonly multi-player. Role play games are usually underpinned by complex statistical models that provide scores for a range of characteristics that determine a character's abilities and weaknesses.

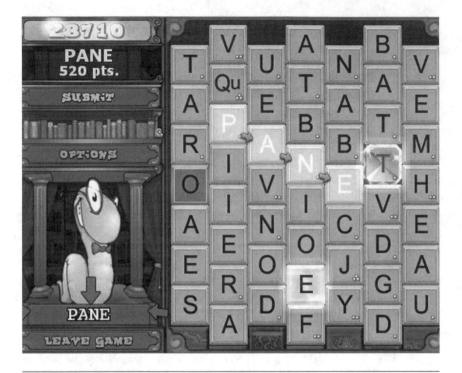

Figure 4.4 *Bookworm* Develops Vocabulary and Spelling (image reproduced with permission of PopCap Games)

In the context of learning, role-playing games are good for providing a context for building collaborative skills, social interaction, negotiation, management of complex systems (e.g. character statistics), strategy, and working through scenarios.

Shooter

Shooter games have the primary aim of using weapons (or sometimes spells and other special abilities) to defeat opponents, although the action is often embedded within a wider narrative context. They are generally played from a first person viewpoint and are played in real time. This is another genre in which multi-player games are common. Shooter games involve a combination of strategy and dexterity, exploring virtual worlds and defeating enemies and targets. Although this is one genre in which it may be argued that there is less applicability to learning in higher education, there are still many skills that can be acquired by playing such games including forward planning, strategizing, and team working.

Figure 4.5 *Guild Wars* is a Popular Massively Multi-player Role-playing Game (image reproduced with permission of ArenaNet)

Sports

Sports games allow the player to simulate taking part in a sporting event or tournament. They are generally based on physical dexterity and interaction with the gaming interface, but in recent years innovations such as dance mats and consoles that use movement-sensitive devices (the most notable example being the Nintendo Wii) have enabled players to actually undertake physical activity while playing. Sporting games can be used to practice the actual skills of a sport (although in the majority of cases this will be a representation through whatever interaction device is available), tactics, rules and the ability to think and make decisions quickly.

Strategy

Strategy games involve the player making strategic decisions within a scenario in order to meet the goal of the game, which is usually completing a level or solving a particular problem. They can involve, for example, movements of armies, progression of a group through various stages of development, management of resources or creation of environments to achieve specific purposes. For example, the strategy game *Age of Empires* involves players progressing their empire through stages of civilization. Many strategy games also have elements of simulation built into them in terms of a complex underlying model of a virtual environment, but will tend to have clear goals. Strategy games can be used for teaching planning, decision-making, testing hypotheses, strategic thinking, management skills and seeing the consequences of actions taken.

Another type of game (which isn't really a genre in itself as there are many different types) that is currently growing in popularity is casual games. These games are usually downloaded from gaming sites rather than being available in shops and are cheaper than traditional entertainment games (or free to play online). Casual games are designed to be played in short bursts rather than for prolonged sessions so are chunked into many small levels that all follow the same pattern, so that they can be played for a few minutes at a time and easily stopped and restarted. These games cater for players who simply want to play a game for a short time and do not want to make any great commitment in terms of time or learning how to play. They have simple game play and comparatively low production values. The rise in the use of casual games shows a movement away from the typical 'hardcore' gamer to a wider demographic, particularly female and older players, which is more typical of the whole university student demographic, and casual games may be most appropriate for fitting into specific segments of teaching time.

Activity: Seeing the Range of Game Genres That Exist

Two of the largest casual gaming sites that exist are

- www.shockwave.com
- www.bigfishgames.com.

Both of these sites contain hundreds of different games in many different genres. Spend half an hour browsing one of these sites and looking at the range of games available.

Can you find an example of each of the genres described previously?

You will see from an exploration of these sites that different games are classified by a variety of different genres, and many games are classified under more than one. While it isn't worth getting too bogged down in classification, an understanding of the different genres that exist is useful when you come to conceptualize and specify your own games.

It is worth noting that the types of game that players favour to play for entertainment and the types that are most appropriate for learning do not always match. In a survey of 200 computing students I found that the most popular game genre, by far, was shooters (although this was closely followed by adventure, strategy and role play).

As well as identifying a range of different genres in order to provide an overview of the potential of computer games for learning, I think that it is helpful to consider, when analysing the value of specific games for learning, some of the different features that are present in different types of games, and which can be present in any genre. These characteristics include the number of players, the platform on which the game is played, and the fidelity of the gaming environment.

The number of players that a game is designed for is an important aspect, particularly in relation to the ideas of learning through the collaborative construction of knowledge and testing ideas on others (see Chapter 3). Games can be designed for a single player (e.g. adventure games or puzzles), multiple players (e.g. online card games) or massively multi-player (in general, it is role-playing and shooter games that are designed for many simultaneous players). There are also games that are designed for multiple players in that they involve turn-taking in the same physical space rather than online interaction (these are usually limited to around four players) and are much more common in console games, which are often designed with social gaming in mind.

The physical platform on which a game is played is also a key distinguishing feature; as well as desktop or laptop computers, games can also be played on a variety of other devices such as gaming consoles, mobile consoles or mobile phones. Different platforms offer a range of different interaction devices including microphones, dance mats and motion sensors, to name but a few. The nature of the interaction device used, the space in which the game is played and whether the computer game medium is static or mobile will also affect the potential of play for learning.

The graphical fidelity of a game and its production value is another key feature – many games for entertainment have extremely high production values with budgets into the millions, while games for education tend to have much smaller budgets and consequently lower production values. Whether a high level of fidelity is required for educational games is a matter of some debate among the educational gaming community. It can be argued that students have high expectations based on their experiences with commercial games and that, in comparison, educational games may be seen as laughable or simply fail to engage. However, I would argue that it is the game design and playability that make a game engaging, and high-end graphics, while adding to immersion, are not the be-all-and-end-all of game design (with the caveat that the graphics are not of such poor quality that they actually distract from the game itself). As mentioned previously, casual games with lower end graphics are becoming increasingly popular, and many popular online games use humour and quirky low-end graphics as a selling point (see, for example, *Kingdom of Loathing* in Figure 4.6). What I do believe is important, however, is that there is thought put into the interaction design for educational games

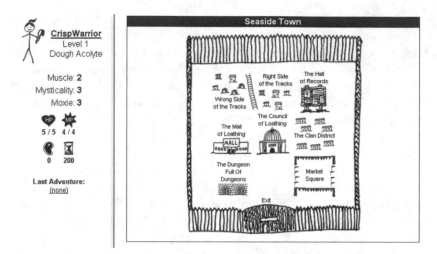

Figure 4.6 *Kingdom of Loathing* (image reproduced with permission of Asymmetric Publications, LLC)

so that they are usable by students and that the interface is not in itself a barrier to play.

Based on this analysis of the different game genres that exist, I am very much of the opinion that certain genres of game are more appropriate for learning in higher education, and that there may be less value in others (although they may be useful in other areas such as children's learning or in skills training). Where I see most potential for the types of learning that take place in higher education is in adventure games for problem-solving, role-playing for collaboration and social interaction, and strategy games for planning, experimenting and creative strategic thinking. I think that there is also a great potential in the use of puzzle games for teaching a range of skills in an engaging way. As well as the question of what games can be used to teach, another approach is to look at what types of learning take place and how they can be facilitated with games; this is discussed in the following section.

Types of Learning that can be Facilitated with Games

In the previous section I discussed a number of different genres of game that exist, and their applicability to teaching and learning in higher education. In this section I will approach the question from a different angle and examine different ways in which types of learning have been categorized, and the different types of game that can be used to facilitate these types.

It has been argued that play is a powerful influence on learning, that the whole purpose of games is to learn, that play is fundamental to our development

(Reiber, 1996) in that it can promote engagement in and mastery of a range of tasks as we mature into adults (Colarusso, 1993). Koster (2005) argues that games are an essential part of the human learning experience, providing the opportunity to safely practise skills like aiming, timing, hunting, strategy and manipulation of power.

Prensky (2006) describes fives levels of learning from video games (although he talks in the context of children's education, I feel that there are lessons to be learned for higher education here). The first level is how to do something (i.e. interact with the system), then players need to learn what to do, that is understand the actual rules of the game. The third level is when players get to grips with the why of the game and develop strategies for achieving the aims (examples given include cause and effect, long-term winning as opposed to short-term gains and complex system behaviours). The fourth learning level is described as the where, understanding the context and value systems intrinsic within the game, and the fifth level is the whether, the ability to make decisions based on the value system imposed by the game. A more comprehensive analysis of what can be learned with games is provided by Gee (2003) who identifies 36 ways in which computer games can support learning, arguing that video games can teach a new kind of literacy, encouraging active and critical thinking while developing identities, contexts, experiences, cultures and social relationships.

Gagné and colleagues (1992) identify five main categories of learning, which are shown with examples in Table 4.1. These categories of learning show a range of elements that could potentially be developed using digital games.

I believe that digital game-based learning can be used to support the development of all five of these capabilities, although in relation to the

Table 4.1 Categories of Learning (adapted from Gagné *et al.*, 1992)

Category	Description
Intellectual skill	Concepts, rules and relationships, and making discriminations (e.g. using algebra to solve a mathematical puzzle).
Cognitive strategy	Personal techniques for thought and action (e.g. developing a mental model of a problem).
Verbal information	Relating facts (e.g. recalling the names of the bones in the hand).
Motor skill	Actions that use the muscles (e.g. dancing).
Attitude	Beliefs and feelings (e.g. choosing to read detective fiction).

constructivist perspective in higher education I would argue that intellectual skills, cognitive strategies and attitudes are most appropriate because they are closely associated with the higher level cognitive skills taught at universities. Bloom (1956) identifies three different levels of learning: the cognitive domain, the affective domain and the psycho-motor domain. Within the cognitive domain he presented a taxonomy of educational objectives, which consists of six levels: knowledge, comprehension, application, analysis, synthesis and evaluation.

Knowledge involves the recall of facts and information, comprehension requires a deeper understanding of the information that allows a person to restate it in their own words, application involves the use of the information or skill in a new situation, analysis involves the deconstruction of the information to determine elements and relationships, synthesis is the reconstruction of the information in a different way and in relation to other concepts, and evaluation involves making judgements about the information. In higher education (particularly in the UK), Bloom's taxonomy is commonly used as a means for determining learning objectives to ensure that they are at an appropriate level, and the focus (particularly in the later years of study) is very much on the higher level outcomes. Anderson and Krathwohl's (2001) revision of Bloom's taxonomy identifies six types of learning in the cognitive domain, each progressively at a higher level: remembering, understanding, applying, analysing, evaluating and creating. The additional idea of creating is about production of new knowledge and, I feel, very much in line with the idea of constructivist learning.

While computer games can be used to support memorization and comprehension for learning in higher education (and indeed drill-and-practice games supporting this type of learning are common in children's learning) it is the higher domains where games can achieve the most potential from a pedagogic point of view. Games that focus on memorization and practice of skills have been used successfully in certain sectors within higher education (for example, in medicine and surgery) but it is by focusing on games that enable students to learn in context, apply their knowledge and test their assumptions, that there is the greatest potential to exploit the characteristics of games for learning.

Another domain in which games can be a very powerful learning tool is the affective, or emotional, domain (Bloom, 1956). The fact that games can immerse players in virtual worlds and alternative realities and can lead to extremely high levels of engagement means also that they have the power to lead the players' emotions, which is a powerful factor in learning. In particular, games that enable the player to empathize with other players or characters, role play is one such example, have the power to harness this potential.

Table 4.2 Examples of Types of Learning with Digital Games

Type of learning	Example
Applying skills	Undertaking a virtual chemistry experiment.
Developing strategies	Working out the best way to defeat an enemy tribe.
Analysing information	Determining how to escape a locked room.
Evaluating situations	Weighing up evidence to find a criminal.
Changing attitudes	Seeing the consequences of polluting a river.
Creating knowledge	Developing new games, modifications or levels.

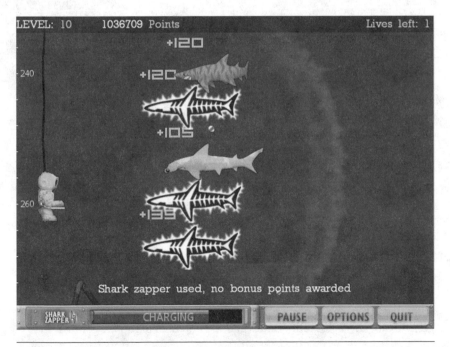

Figure 4.7 *Typer Shark* (image reproduced with permission of PopCap Games)

Table 4.2 draws together these theories to show key areas of learning in higher education where I believe games have the most potential for influencing learning, with examples of how they could be achieved using digital games.

Although the focus here is on development of higher level skills, I acknowledge that there are still good examples of appropriate uses of games for skills such as recall and those that develop motor skills. A good example of this is the game Typer Shark (see Figure 4.7) that provides a more engaging way of supporting the necessary practice required to master touch-typing.

This game is, I think, a particularly good example because the skill to be learned (typing) is directly equivalent to the skill practised during the game. The examples of this type are limited because of the limited nature of interaction devices available.

Activity: Analysing the Types of Learning that Happen in Games

Select one of the three games described in the introductory chapter (or another computer game you are familiar with if you prefer).

Now spend 20–30 minutes playing the game while thinking about what you might be learning while playing.

Note down examples of the types of learning described in Table 4.2 above.

Depending on the game you have selected, you may find that there is very little learning of this kind. The majority of games are designed for entertainment and what makes a fun game does not necessarily make a good game for higher level learning. An understanding of what types of learning can be facilitated with certain games, and an ability to analyse games for the types of learning they might contain is, in itself, a useful activity for understanding the potential of learning with games.

New Directions in Digital Games for Learning

While discussing different types of digital games for learning, I wanted to take the opportunity to look at two of the new areas of digital game-based learning that I think will grow and be influential in the sector in the coming years. The areas that I think are of particular interest for higher education (and learning in general) are alternate reality games and the potential of mobile gaming.

Alternate Reality Games

Alternate reality games (ARGs) are a comparatively recent type of game where an underlying narrative unfolds over time as players complete a range of collaborative challenges, both online and in the real world. The first fully formed ARG is widely held to be a game called 'The Beast' that was created in 2001 as a promotional vehicle for the Steven Spielberg movie *AI* (Hon, 2005). Sean Stewart (2006), lead writer of 'The Beast', suggests four characteristics of ARGs:

- an ongoing storyline is fragmented, which the players assemble, piecing together the narrative from multiple sources as the game unfolds;
- use of many different media types to act as a delivery mechanism for the game, such as print, telephone, email, web pages, television and advertising;
- a collaborative environment in which players are required to cooperate to solve the puzzles;
- an environment where the audience interact with the game world and are responsible for shaping it.

Alternate reality games provide an authentic context and purpose for activity, both online and in the real world; they are fundamentally collaborative in nature; and by presenting a series of challenges and an unfolding narrative they create puzzlement and mystery. ARGs also generally take place over several weeks, or even months, providing the space for reflection.

Alternate reality games also start to blur the line between player and game designer, because participants are involved throughout in shaping the story and contributing to the narrative in a way that goes beyond simply playing the game. A common feature of ARGs is their ability to create self-sustaining communities with established players supporting and mentoring new players – this feature has potential within higher education to provide a framework for peer mentoring. A further advantage of ARGs over other types of computer game, because they rely predominantly on existing web technologies, is that they do not require the same level of production value, technical ability, time or expense to produce. This makes them a much more practical and feasible game-based option for education. In addition, because players experience a number of different types of media there is the added outcome of familiarizing them with a wide range of internet technologies. Moseley (2008) presents seven pedagogic benefits of alternate reality games:

- Facilitation of problem-solving at all levels in the form of graded challenges, and enabling students to pick up their own starting levels of competence and start from there.
- Steady and ongoing progress and tangible rewards (usually in terms of a leader board, prize artefacts such as badges or a grand prize). There is also potential for relating these rewards to assessment.
- They employ narrative devices such as characters, plot and story (which don't have to be fictional or fantastic but can fit into real-world themes such as history or news) to stimulate curiosity and engagement.

- Players have the power to influence the outcomes of the game, in terms of plot direction, storyline and game play. This increases engagement and their stake in and ownership of the game.
- Regular delivery of problems and events, which is key to maintaining engagement, allows the game to be modified as it progresses, and provides space between events for students to reflect.
- There is the potential for a large, active community to be built around the game, with a group that is self-supporting and provides scaffolding and advice for new players.
- They are based on simple, existing technologies, and because they rely predominantly on existing web technologies, they do not require high-end production values and therefore do not need the same levels of technical expertise or expense to produce as commercial games. This makes them a much more practical and feasible game-based option for education.

Some commercial games also make good use of the wider online environment as part of the game, blending the game world and the real world. *In Memoriam* is an example of such a game, where players have to solve a series of riddles to catch a serial killer by carrying out investigations online, emailing characters and analysing rich media.

An example of using an ARG in higher education is the Alternate Reality Games for Orientation, Socialization and Induction (ARGOSI) project, a joint project between Manchester Metropolitan University and the University of Bolton. The project aimed to provide an alternative to traditional student induction by developing an ARG framework for mapping learning objectives to game challenges (Whitton *et al.*, 2008). A game called *ViolaQuest* was developed in which players had to solve a variety of challenges to find pieces of a map that would provide a clue to a 'hidden machine'. Solving these challenges would also help the players find their way around Manchester, meet other people, and develop their information literacy skills.

Although there are clearly benefits to the notion of using alternate reality games in education, there are also a range of potential drawbacks. Relying as they do on the imaginative use of existing low-tech tools such as blogs, social networking sites, email and 'the real world' to create the gaming environment, the development of an ARG can be relatively straightforward compared to the typical development cycles of traditional computer games. However, because they rely on an engaging narrative interlinked with a robust series of challenges they are still a non-trivial undertaking requiring a broad cross-section of creative skills in web development, game design, graphic design and storytelling, as well as the necessary subject expertise to ensure that challenges are appropriately associated with learning outcomes (i.e. students will achieve the intended learning outcomes from playing the game, as well as the gaming outcomes).

From a logistic point of view it is difficult to run an ARG with too few or too many participants. The game needs a critical mass of players in order to make the collaborative game play possible and to allow the social network of players to develop naturally (with the ultimate goal that it will become self-supporting). During the running time of an ARG a core team is needed to monitor the game interaction, reveal clues and pieces of the story, create blog postings and interact with the players in many other ways; if there were too many participants this would require a level of administration that could not necessarily be delivered.

Another consideration is that the use of ARGs in an educational context may always remain niche. A pilot scheme at the University of Brighton that also used an ARG to support student induction concluded that the game 'provides an interesting alternative to existing mechanisms for introducing students to certain types of information or services. This format does not appeal to all students, but is very effective for those that like it' (Piatt, 2007: 2). It is important to consider how many players are required before an ARG becomes a cost-effective tool. This game is described in more detail in Case Study 1.

A final point is the relative newness of the genre in terms of research and the lack of academic papers published in the area. As ARGs are a comparatively recent trend, originating from the commercial and grassroots gaming communities, so far very little academic analysis has been carried out within the genre. If they are to be considered as an effective pedagogic tool in the field of higher education, and achieve mainstream acceptance, it is important that their effectiveness in terms of learning and student engagement is rigorously researched by the academic community.

Mobile Gaming

A second area that I think has great potential to benefit education in coming years is the use of mobile and handheld technologies for gaming, such as mobile phones. The decreasing costs of technology coupled with increasing processing power and the growing ownership of handheld devices now creates a real possibility for making use of mobile devices for learning.

Mobile gaming, like alternate reality games, has the advantage of being able to integrate the real and online worlds, and make the most of the fact that the location of a person can be tracked in real-time and that they can be communicated with on the move. Kolo and Baur make the point that mobile phone games cannot compete in terms of user-interface, graphics, processing power or memory but instead need to focus on what they do best: 'new ideas that exploit the unique properties of mobility, time, location-awareness and instant connectivity, along with the ability to deliver on-demand content to a device profoundly linked to a single person and usually being carried at all times' (Kolo & Baur, 2008: 29).

The following two examples of the use of mobile games for learning are both taken from the sphere of children's learning but, I feel, exemplify principles that could equally well be applied to learning in higher education. The Savannah project developed a mobile game to support children's understanding of animal behaviour (Facer *et al.*, 2004), and a mobile game called *Frequency 1550* was developed to support students learning about the history of medieval Amsterdam (Huizenga *et al.*, 2008).

In the Savannah project children's activity takes place on a playing field, where they play at being a pride of lions, interacting with a virtual savannah through personal digital assistants (PDAs) equipped with global positioning systems (GPS). This location-awareness enables the players to experience the threats and opportunities real lions might experience through audio, textual and graphical feedback as they move through the savannah. The real-world play is coupled with reflective time where players can discuss their actions and the game play. The *Frequency 1550* game supports the learning of medieval history as players walk through Amsterdam and use their phones to answer questions on the medieval buildings or places they pass. The real-world players are supported by other players at a central base with laptops who have to communicate and share information in order to complete collaborative assignments.

These two examples show the two key features of mobile gaming for learning: the use of location-aware technology and the potential for collaboration. As yet underexplored in relation to learning, these are two aspects of mobile gaming that I believe will grow and greatly support real-world learning in the coming years. However, mobile gaming often involves the use of technology owned by the students, which can lead to inequity of access as well as a potential unwillingness on the part of learners to use personal technologies in this way.

This chapter, the last on theory, has aimed to consider the types of games that are best for learning and the types of learning that are most suited to the use of games in higher education. In the next part of the book we move on to look at some of the practical implementation issues of actually embedding the use of computer games in higher education.

Chapter Summary

This chapter first presented an overview of game genres (adventure, platform, puzzle, role play, shooter, sports and strategy) and highlighted adventure, role play and strategy as those most suited for learning in higher education.

The second section looked at theories of learning in terms of what is most appropriate to be taught with games in the higher education context and presented six areas that I believe are those most appropriate to be taught with computer games in this context. These are: the application of skills, development of strategies, analysis of information, evaluation of situations, changing attitudes and creating knowledge.

In the final section of the chapter I introduced and described two emerging areas of gaming for learning – alternate reality games and mobile gaming – where I feel there is, as yet, much untapped potential in the field.

Further Reading

J. P. Gee (2003). *What Video Games have to Teach us about Learning and Literacy*. New York: Palgrave Macmillan. An in-depth analysis of the potential of computer games for learning.

K. Oxland (2004). *Gameplay and Design*. Harlow: Addison-Wesley. Chapter 17 gives a short overview of the future of computer games.

M. J. P. Wolf (2001). Genre and the video game. In M. J. P. Wolf (Ed.), *The Medium of the Video Game* (pp. 113–34). Austin, TX: University of Texas Press. This comprehensive discussion presents over 40 different genres of game.

PART II

Practice

CHAPTER 5

Integrating Digital Games Into the Curriculum

In this chapter I review the practical issues that need to be considered when analysing the context of learning and discuss various ways to integrate digital games into real learning and teaching situations.

After covering the pedagogic benefits of learning with digital games in the previous part of the book, I hope you are now someway to being convinced that computer games are a valid way to teach in higher education. I move on in this chapter to look at the practical issues and constraints you need to consider before starting to design a game for your own context. At this stage I examine the practical issues that arise with the use of digital games for teaching in typical higher education institutions. The chapter then goes on to provide a framework for undertaking a contextual analysis of your own situation as a basis for considering what types of game might be the most appropriate and productive. Finally, the chapter presents six different ways in which digital games can be integrated into a higher education curriculum, with a discussion of the benefits and disadvantages of each.

Analysing the Learning Context

Here I look at some of the practicalities of using games in real teaching and learning situations, and address some of the first things you need to think about when integrating a learning game into your own teaching. I am assuming at this point that you may have in mind an area in which you would like to introduce game-based learning in your own practice and would encourage you to work through the activities with this in mind. At the end of the chapter you will have a more fully formed idea of an area you want to address and the constraints that exist. In the next chapter I will take this forward to look at developing a game specification.

There are four areas that it is useful to consider before you actually start specifying what any game might look like: the people involved, organizational issues, the environment and nature of the technology. I think these are particularly important in terms of examining what is feasible and practical in any given situation. While it is all very well to want to use a high-end bespoke game over the course of a year, if the constraints of timetabling, access to technology and teaching spaces available don't match then it isn't going to happen.

People

The first aspect to consider is the people who will be involved in designing, running, playing and supporting the game. What are their levels of computing experience? What educational and cultural backgrounds do they come from? What are their attitudes to technology and games? How might these factors affect any game you want to use? This includes technical and educational staff involved in development, teaching staff, students and any other technical or administrative staff involved in implementing the game. It is important to think at the start about who might be affected, and whether the appropriate expertise and goodwill are available.

Students will be those most affected by using the game, and considering the nature of the student population and the acceptability of using a game is essential. This is particularly true in the context of mature adult learners, who may have many conflicting pressures on their time, are possibly less likely to be interested in or motivated to play games for their own sake, and may in fact regard them as frivolous and a waste of time.

It is also very important to consider the range of accessibility issues that students may have with digital games for learning. There may be limitations because of disabilities, access to equipment or lack of previous experience using a particular gaming genre. It is key to consider how a game would be inaccessible to someone with a visual impairment (e.g. is it all based on pictures?), a hearing impairment (e.g. is there an alternative way to deal with sounds?), a mobility impairment (e.g. are specific keystroke combinations required?) or a cognitive disability (e.g. are there large amounts of text that need to be read onscreen?).

Organization

The second aspect to think about is how a course is currently organized, when teaching takes place and how it is timetabled. For example, are timetables fixed and does teaching happen in set rooms that might restrict the use of a game? Consider also how long a course takes to run in total and how much of that time is available for using the game and associated activities, and how this fits into the overall teaching calendar.

Environment

This heading covers the environmental constraints associated with the use of game-based learning, such as where the learning will take place, where teaching takes place and the types of rooms and equipment that are available. You should also think about the potential noise levels and impact on other learners, particularly if you are going to be having a large number of students collaborating. This, of course, will be an issue for any collaborative learning activity, but because digital game-based learning often happens in computer labs, which can be open-plan and are not always designed for this type of learning in a way that, say seminar rooms are, this can be an issue.

Technology

Also crucial to consider is available access to technology, both for teachers and students, and the types of hardware and software that you want to use. It is important to ensure that access is equitable for all students; for example, if you are expecting students to work on their own at home, can you be sure that they have access to the appropriate hardware and networks? You also need to consider whether all machines are capable of running the software you plan to use. Don't assume that all users will be running the latest version of Windows – they may be using older versions, other operating systems or types of computer, and a whole range of different internet browsing software. Talking over these issues with a local technician or member of IT support staff at an early stage is invaluable.

You should also think about whether there will be institutional barriers to using the technology, such as firewalls or restrictive network implementations, whether the technology you intend to use will be capable of running the type of software you want, and whether any peripheral devices required (e.g. webcams, microphones, speakers) will be available. The answers to these questions will depend very much on the individual institution and the context of use.

Throughout this chapter and the next I will use an example of a game I developed for teaching basic collaborative skills for computing students that, I hope, will exemplify the points made here. The game, called *The Time Capsule,* asked students to take on the role of one of four characters and take part in a negotiation exercise to agree on six items to be included within a time capsule. The final design of the game is shown in Figure 5.1.

The Time Capsule was used with first-year computing students for a single hour session in a computing laboratory as part of a larger course introducing them to a range of skills that would be useful at university. Table 5.1 shows a contextual analysis undertaken before development of the game.

From this analysis several constraints were highlighted, the most important being the very limited teaching time available. With a maximum of one hour total teaching time (less if you count the time for students to move between classes) I decided that a game that took more than 40 minutes would not be appropriate. As I did not have definite numbers or names for each class I could not design a game that required set numbers to play. The physical environment of a noisy computer lab also acted as a constraint as it made the potential for face-to-face group work and discussion limited. On the positive side, the student group was one likely to find games acceptable and have experience in using them and the computing facilities available were consistent and high quality. In addition, I had the appropriate expertise to develop a game myself, so this made more options available to me in terms of game design.

This is, of course, a very simplistic example provided to show how an analysis of the learning context might work. Providing as much detail as you can at this stage will really help your thinking when you come to specify the type of game you require later on.

Hopefully, after seeing how you can undertake a contextual analysis for yourself this will have helped you to identify some of the constraints and opportunities that exist in your own situation. It is also worth thinking at this

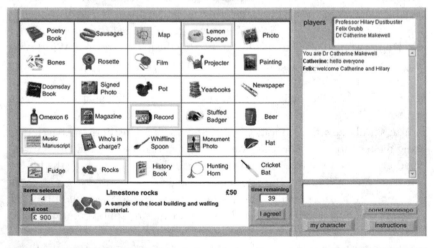

Figure 5.1 *The Time Capsule* Game

Table 5.1 Contextual Analysis for *The Time Capsule*

People	Organization
Students are first-year undergraduates undertaking a variety of computing-related degrees. It is likely that games will be acceptable and that they will be experienced with technology and games.	A single hour of teaching time is available.
	There are six one-hour slots over the course of a week with approximately 25 students attending each class.
	There is no flexibility.
I have experience of teaching group skills and programming expertise.	There are around 150 students in the class as a whole.
I will need to involve the other teachers on the course to ensure that they are happy with using a game.	
Environment	**Technology**
All teaching takes place in a computing lab.	Each student will have access to a PC running Windows XP and Internet Explorer.
A data projector is available in each room.	The network is fast and there should be no bandwidth limitations.
The labs are open-plan and generally noisy. Teaching will be taking place in labs on either side.	All students will need an ID to access the system.

point about what might be constraints in the short term (e.g. fixed timetable) but might be overcome in the medium to long term. The following section looks at the different ways that you could integrate games into a curriculum, and this analysis should give you some idea about what is achievable in your context. Before I go on to talk about these options there are a few other practical considerations that I think are worth talking about, as they may be aspects that you need to consider.

Setting Expectations

Setting student expectations as to the point and value of a game is key to its acceptability and success, particularly when working with more mature adult learners with time pressures and a greater need to be convinced of the benefits of learning with computer games. It is important to provide a clear rationale for why the game is being used – and why it is the best option for learning in this context. It is also important to set ground rules for communication (e.g. what is appropriate etiquette?) and collaboration (e.g. what is collaboration and what is cheating?). Being clear about whether and how the game will be assessed early on is also of importance (assessment will be examined in more detail in Chapter 7).

Activity: Undertaking a Contextual Analysis

The headings below show some of the questions you might want to consider when analysing the constraints of your own teaching and learning context.

People
Will game-based learning be acceptable to your students?
What is their previous experience with technology and games?
What available expertise do you have?
Who do you need to get involved with developing and running a game?

Organization
How much time is available?
Is there a fixed timetable?
Is there any flexibility?
How many students will take part?

Environment
Where will teaching take place?
What equipment will be available?
Are there any noise constraints?

Technology
What hardware is available?
Are there any network limitations?
What software (e.g. operating systems, internet browsers) is available?

In your own context, take 20 minutes now to answer as many of these questions as you can. How might this constrain or support the types of game that you could plan to use?

Learning to Play the Game

It is also important to consider how long it might take students to learn how to play any computer game as well as actually undertaking learning through playing the game. This includes aspects such as mastering the game interface, navigation around the environment, understanding what is expected to happen and what they are expected to do. Don't underestimate how long these acclimatization processes take and how important they are to get right so that students are comfortable playing the game. How much time you give to allow students to learn to play the game and familiarize themselves with the interface will, of course, depend on the total time available for using the game.

Safety

There may be issues of personal safety if learners are being asked to work outside the normal teaching environment, particularly if students are encouraged to meet and work with other students who may be unknown to them or they have only met in the course of an online game. It is good practice to provide information about personal safety online in situations like this.

In the following sections I examine different ways in which digital games can be integrated into learning and teaching in higher education. First I explore briefly the differences between using games in face-to-face and online distance contexts, before describing six different models of integration for you to consider for application to your own practice. These sections should help to generate ideas about the wide variety of ways in which computer games can potentially be used as part of a higher education curriculum.

Gaming Online and Face-to-Face

The physical context in which computer games can be used may vary greatly. For example, interactive games such as quizzes can be facilitated in large lecture theatres using interactive voting systems or mobile phones. Digital games can be used in computer labs with individuals, pairs or small groups on each computer; they can be used in the real world on devices such as mobile phones, in face-to-face workshops followed by opportunities to input decisions online, using individual handheld console devices in tutorials, or by students carrying out game-play and collaborative activities remotely at a distance from one another as part of an online course. There are lots of opportunities to be creative here in the ways that we think about using games in higher education. One key difference, however, is the nature of the interaction between students that are interacting fully online and those that have the opportunity to communicate face-to-face. In the next section I will highlight some of these differences and their implications.

There are a number of differences that I feel are worth highlighting between the use of games in a face-to-face teaching setting and using them at a distance in a fully online context. These include issues of accessing the game or installing it, support required, communication, the differences between synchronous and asynchronous play, anonymity and identity, cheating, learner autonomy and timing and location.

It is more difficult for students to get started in online contexts than it is when working face-to-face with a teacher. In the latter situation they will be able to ask for help from the teacher and other students if they have problems understanding what they are meant to do in the game or how they are supposed to interact with the interface. In an online distance context this is not so easy to achieve and students who have initial difficulties may quickly lose interest or become demotivated. It is important therefore to ensure that initial support for getting started is robust and there are alternative back-up mechanisms (e.g. telephone support) for those who have problems. Ongoing and accessible technical support is vital for online students. The same is true for ongoing support throughout the game; again in online contexts it is important to ensure that appropriate technical help is available at all times. This can include context-sensitive help, hints, support groups and a telephone helpline. Access to the teacher and support throughout the use of the game – as in any form of online teaching – is key.

In a face-to-face session it is possible for the teacher to have a great deal more control over the types of communication that take place (be they verbal or online) but in a fully online situation – even if you provide specific communication tools – you can never be sure that students are using the tools stipulated or using them in the way that you might expect. Offering students a range of tools for interaction (e.g. chat rooms, instant messaging, social networking sites, gaming community forums, telephone) and not being prescriptive about how they interact is helpful. At a distance it can also be more difficult to organize students to communicate and play with each other synchronously, so it is worth considering more flexible asynchronous alternatives so that the unavailability of one student does not limit the opportunity for another to progress.

The level of autonomy required for online students is necessarily higher than for those that are studying face-to-face (this is true of all online learning, not just games) and therefore setting expectations, time management and study planning around the use of the game is important. Students are likely to be more flexible in their study patterns and study at times and locations to suit themselves. In a face-to-face context it is possible to have a great deal more control about when and where students interact with a game. At a distance you cannot make any assumptions about the time of day that they might be using it (and students may not even be located within the same time zone), so you should bear this in mind when designing activities that require actions to happen at particular times (e.g. where a game 'day' is linked to the real 24-hour day) or locations (e.g. where students are expected to use an artefact in the physical environment).

In online games there is often the option for students to play anonymously and take on different roles and online identities. This can have the advantage that they feel less constrained and more open but also the potential disadvantage that they can engage in abusive and unconstructive behaviours without discovery. Setting of community ground rules on anonymity and behaviour is essential in an online context. It is also much more difficult to recognize and deal with cheating in a distance context, as it is difficult to guarantee that a player is who they say they are or to gauge how much of their input is their own. However, I would argue that a well-designed educational game should not be focused on winning as such but more on collaboration and achieving group aims and objectives, so that a player who cheats is not really achieving anything for themselves or for the group. The way that assessment is designed is a key factor here (this is covered in greater detail in Chapter 7).

Models of Integration

There are many ways in which computer games can be embedded into a course, and in this section I will describe six different models of integration. There are, of course, many variations of these, but I think that these models provide a good overview of the options available. Which ones you will be able to use in any given situation will depend a lot on the factors described in the first section of this chapter as well as the regulations and quality assurance processes at an individual institution. Whether there is scope for changing timetables, teaching mode, location and assessment will all influence the degree to which each of the models can be implemented.

Single-Session Game

Probably the most straightforward, and least intrusive, way of introducing computer game-based learning, this involves simply using a game in a single teaching session to cover particular learning outcomes for that session. The advantages of this approach is that you can use it to build confidence in game-based learning – both for yourself and for your students – without taking a major risk if anything doesn't work as planned. It can be a way to energize a class and provide an alternative approach catering for different types of learning style. The disadvantage is really one of time: it can be difficult to get the most out of a game when it is used in a single session, and there is the overhead of finding or developing a suitable game, setting expectations, teaching students how to use the game and briefing, which is relatively high when the game is only going to be used on one occasion.

An example of this approach is *The Time Capsule* game introduced earlier. The game was designed to fit into a one-hour teaching session in a computer lab and lasted approximately 40 minutes; there was a follow-up activity (also included in the one-hour time slot) in which students were asked to discuss and reflect in their groups about what had happened in the game and how they had worked together as a team.

Multiple-Session Game

This is essentially one step up from the single-session game, where the game is used as a direct replacement for two or more teaching sessions. This has the advantages of still being relatively low risk while making better use of the time spent to learn the game; it also better allows for the integration of other activities and reflection between sessions. However, the disadvantage is that the same players may not be available at each session so group interaction has to be carefully designed, and if the game is used in many sessions – particularly if it is not explicitly related to the assessment – some students may feel that it is constituting too large a proportion of the course as a whole. Again, there is a need to set students' expectations and clearly articulate the benefits of any game as an effective way to teach in that situation. Examples of a multiple-session game in practice are provided in Case Studies 3 and 4.

Optional Game Activity

A third alternative is to use a computer game as an optional add-on activity. This is a low-risk strategy as it will not be replacing any teaching sessions, and may engage students who would otherwise not be engaged (although it could be argued that it is those students who are already engaged who are more likely to take part). As well as the increased overhead on the teacher, in terms of time taken to develop and run the game, the disadvantages are that there may be difficulty timetabling out of established contact hours, some students may be unable to attend because of work or home pressures and feel excluded, and, because it is an optional activity, take-up may be low.

Embedded Game

A fourth option is to use a digital game in such a way that it provides the opportunity to reassess the way in which learning, teaching and assessment are carried out on a course, with the potential for completely restructuring the course. This involves embedding a game completely within the curriculum and making it the focus for teaching – an approach that has much in common with problem-based learning. The advantages are that the use of the game, associated activities and assessment can be purposefully aligned in such a way that the game is the focus of the whole course. Disadvantages are that students who do not value the game-based approach may be alienated, it is more risky since the whole course depends upon the use of the game and it may be more difficult to make the approach fit within university regulations and quality standards. It may also be more difficult to make a game match a set of learning outcomes in an existing course than to develop a course from scratch based around a game.

An example of the embedded approach took place at Napier University, where the commercial educational game Marketplace was used to develop a course in the application of marketing theory. Marketplace is a team-based game that is run over a number of decision periods, where each team of students has to develop a marketing strategy for a computer firm, making decisions each period on items such as pricing, products and advertising and gaining feedback on the market position of each of the companies at the end of each period. The whole course was based on the game, with each tutorial session being used for groups to analyse their current positions and make decisions for the forthcoming period, with support from the lecturer who was present at each tutorial. An early formative assessment took the form of a presentation to the 'Board of Directors' and the final evaluation consisted of a group analysis of the decisions made, an individual articulation of ongoing strategy and an individual reflective account of the team-working processes. An example of the use of an embedded game is provided in Case Studies 2 and 5.

Online Game

The fifth option is the use of a fully online game as part of a blended or fully online course. In this case the students do not need to meet each other face-to-face at all but play entirely online either synchronously or independently. These types of games could involve the use of fully online virtual worlds or could involve players working independently and supporting others to share resources and hints. In this instance, building in methods of communication and backup when there is not a lecturer physically present is vital.

Mixed Reality Game

A mixed reality game uses elements of the online environment as well as the face-to-face, often integrating mobile technologies such as mobile phones or other handheld devices. Alternate reality games (ARGs) are a good example of this type of game and combine real-world and online challenges to provide an engaging, interactive and fun experience for the players (more detail on alternate reality games is provided in Chapter 4). The rationale behind the use of ARGs is that the use of problem-based, experiential and collaborative activities in alternate reality games makes them ideally suited to teaching in higher education; particularly as they enable players to become involved in both playing the game and shaping the narrative as it emerges. Participation in the game also provides a useful pretext for social interaction and collaboration. Unlike high-fidelity digital games, using advanced 3D graphics or virtual environments, ARGs are typically implemented using inexpensive technologies such as blogs, social networking sites and other web-based tools, which makes their potential in education viable financially and technically. An example of an alternate reality game for induction is provided in Case Study 1.

Activity: Selecting an Appropriate Integration Strategy

Take ten minutes now to reflect on your own circumstances and the type of game you might like to use.

What areas could you like to use a game to teach (what are the learning objective you would like to address)?

What implementation strategy do you think would be appropriate in the first instance?

Are there any particular issues or constraints that need to be addressed? Can you identify individuals in your institution who could give you advice or support in addressing them?

From your analysis of appropriate integration strategies in your situation, you may feel that the issues and constraints identified are insurmountable at this stage. If you are new to digital games for learning, I would suggest opting for one of the lower risk strategies as a trial in the first instance. As you gain experience, and the value of your game becomes apparent (or conversely it becomes clear that this is not an appropriate strategy), it will be easier for you to make decisions on how to proceed.

In this chapter I have introduced a way to analyse the contextual factors that influence how a game might be used and considered a range of practical issues that must be taken into account when using digital games in learning and teaching in higher education. In the next chapter I will move on to look at how to design a game specification, taking into account the pedagogic aspects of game design and drawing on good practice.

Chapter Summary

The chapter started by looking at four areas that may constrain how games can be integrated into a teaching and learning situation – people, organization, environment and technology – and provided a framework for contextual analysis.

The second part of the chapter considered differences in the way in which game-based learning is implemented in online and face-to-face contexts, looking particularly at aspects such as getting started, support required, communication, autonomy and identity.

Finally, six models of integration were presented and discussed: using single-session game, using a game over multiple sessions, employing an optional game activity, embedding a game throughout the curriculum, using a fully online game, and implementing a mixed reality game.

CHAPTER **6**

Designing a Digital Game for Learning

> In this chapter I introduce some pedagogic design considerations, describe guidelines for the development of learning games for higher education and present a method for developing a game concept specification.

I look first at how digital games can be designed to meet specified learning objectives, how they can be designed to be collaborative and how activities can be designed to support the game. A consideration in the use of games in university education is the overheads in terms of development or modification and the expertise required, so I then provide a brief overview of the options available for acquiring or creating games. The chapter continues with a discussion of six guidelines that emerged from my own research on the factors that make digital games effective for learning from a constructivist perspective and concludes by providing a framework for specifying a game to use in your own teaching situation.

Pedagogic Design Considerations

Ensuring that game design is in accord with desired learning objectives from a game is one of the crucial elements of design, and this is addressed first in this section. Collaboration is an important aspect of game design from a social constructivist perspective so I go on to look at the variety of ways in which collaboration can be built into game design. Lastly I discuss the need for wraparound activities for briefing, debriefing and reflection and present a number of different activities that you could consider for use in your own practice.

Aligning Game Play and Learning Objectives

Educational games are generally designed to facilitate some kind of learning objectives, that is, what it is intended that students will learn from playing the game. Games that are designed purely for entertainment focus on playability and fun as their core objectives (although learning may take place, this is incidental to the game play). As players progress through a game there are various goals intrinsic to the game, for example moving through levels, gaining points, unlocking secret areas. A key challenge when designing a game for learning is ensuring that the goals within the game support the learning objectives and do not detract from them. For example, if in a game it is quicker to progress by random clicking than by actually engaging with the game, then the game goals may be easily achieved but there will be little learning taking place. On the other hand, if a game is designed in such a way that progress necessitates engagement with the intended learning objectives then it is much more likely to be a successful learning tool. A computer game can be extremely motivating and engaging for students, but if it doesn't teach what they are meant to be learning in a particular syllabus, then it will not be educationally effective in that context (although it may still teach valuable skills).

In my opinion, it is this mapping of learning and gaming outcomes that fundamentally determines whether a game will be an effective learning tool or not. When you begin to think about using games for learning, start with the learning objectives you want the students to achieve during the session, course or elements of the course – which can then form part of a design specification for the game you want to use. It is very easy to find a game that you think would be good, and to rationalize why it should be used, even though the learning outcomes aren't really addressed. Once you are clear about the learning outcomes, think next about the types of activity that you would normally undertake with students in order to meet those outcomes. How might these types of activities be embedded within a game – this is the point where you can be creative and brainstorm different ways in which these activities could be modified or embedded within a game format. Table 6.1 shows a mapping of the learning outcomes from the *Time Capsule* game (described in Chapter 5).

Undertaking a mapping exercise of this kind will give you a good idea, before you start to look for or develop an appropriate game, of the types of game activities and interactions that are appropriate for your given teaching situation. Once you have some idea of the types of gaming activities that would be appropriate to meet the learning objectives, you will have a basis for

Table 6.1 Mapping of Learning Objectives to Game Activity for *The Time Capsule*

Learning objectives	Learning activities	Game activities
Be able to communicate successfully with others.	Sharing information with others. Listening to what others have to say.	Each player has a different background and needs that they have to communicate. Each player must understand the needs of other players.
Be able to successfully work together and reach effective decisions.	Make a group decision where members have to reach consensus. Members need to negotiate on conflicting goals and interests.	Players have to make a decision as a group to which they all agree. There are constraints that exist in the game that make this non-trivial. Each player must be prepared to compromise on some issues to complete the game.
Be aware of the elements that make a group effective.	Reflection on group communication and decision-making processes.	Reflection on group communication and decision-making processes.

reassessing your requirements and evaluating the appropriateness of a given game.

As I said earlier, one of the hardest practical issues to address is ensuring alignment between game activities and learning outcomes. However, if the game itself does not meet – or fully meet – all of the desired learning outcomes, this is not the end of the world. You should view the use of the game as part of a learning package and remember that it can be augmented through a range of additional activities surrounding the game. In the case of the *Time Capsule*, the third learning outcome was not actually built into the game but was met in a reflective activity that took place after the game itself had finished.

It is also important to note that not all learning outcomes are necessarily suitable or appropriate to be taught with digital games and if you are really struggling to conceive appropriate gaming activities then it could well be the case that a game is not appropriate in that instance.

Hopefully by undertaking this activity you will appreciate the importance – and difficulty – of mapping game activities on to learning objectives. Taking the time to write down and think about this alignment is, I feel, the single most important activity you can do to ensure that your game is appropriate for learning what you want your students to learn. You may also find that you cannot think of any appropriate gaming activities in your case, and this is a

Activity: Mapping Learning Objectives

Select a lesson that you are familiar with that has three to five learning objectives.

For each learning objective write down the activities that students would normally undertake to meet that objective.

Now, for each objective, think about the types of interaction that might take place in a game that would be equivalent to these learning activities. Write down your ideas. (Don't worry if you're a bit short of ideas at this stage, we'll be revisiting this mapping later on in the chapter when we look at creating a more complete game specification.)

Is any particular genre of game suggesting itself to you at this stage?

good way of identifying learning outcomes that may be problematic and need to be addressed in an activity external to the game. Remember also that games are not necessarily an appropriate way to teach everything – if you are finding it really difficult to think of a gaming activity then it could be that a game is not suitable in this instance.

Supporting Collaboration

I would strongly argue that the most effective educational games are those which involve some aspect of collaboration with others, allowing students to work together, learn from others and test their understandings (this thinking is very much in line with the social constructivist paradigm discussed in Chapter 3). However, this does not necessarily require collaboration to take place during the time the game is actually played, and any collaboration does not need to be online. There are a range of options available for supporting collaboration with digital games, a selection of which are described in the box.

There are other variants but those described here should serve to provide a taster of the range of options available for building collaborative learning experiences. In whatever way a game is designed, be it with people working as individuals, or as part of a team, aiming to complete a challenge or compete against other players, you should also consider the level of dependency that students have on one another and the effects on one learner of non-engagement by others. If you want collaboration to take place synchronously then it is important to consider the number of players you have and whether you can guarantee that they will all be available at any given time. If there is a large number of players then there may always be people available to play with and it doesn't matter exactly how many players there are (see e.g. the popular multi-

Synchronous multi-player online games allow collaboration to take place in real-time as the game progresses. This can be through the use of in-game chat or voice communication, or by using additional software such as multi-party audio or video conferencing.

Asynchronous multi-player online games happen asynchronously by turn-taking, with one person making a move and then waiting for the next person (or group) to make theirs. Games of this type can be slow, however, and involve one person waiting for the next person to make a move, which forces time interdependency between players.

Multi-user games involve turn-taking in the same physical space, e.g. console games where each player takes a turn and then watches as the other players take their turns.

Single player games with synchronous online communication where players can discuss the game as it progresses, e.g. online adventure games where players can talk and offer each other hints. The communication can again be built into the game or be part of a third-party application.

Single-player games with face-to-face communication where two or more players collaborate in the same physical space, e.g. players sitting next to one another to develop solutions in a strategy game.

Single-player games with community support are played individually but have associated online communities and synchronous messaging offering hints, help and support.

Single-player games with face-to-face reflection are again played individually but are supported by break-out activities and discussion with others.

Team games where groups of people work together (either online or offline) to achieve the goals of the game and compete against other teams.

player game *iSketch* shown in Figure 6.1) but if a specific number of players is required (as in *Mini Golf* in Figure 6.2) then there need to be systems in place to allow players to wait until the requisite number of people are available (in this case there is a holding room where players can wait, chat and approach others to play).

In the case of the *Time Capsule* I wanted to design a game where collaboration could take place synchronously and, because it was to be used in a classroom situation, I would have some control over forming groups and ensuring that they could all access the same game. However, I could never be sure exactly how many students would be present in a given session so could not have a set

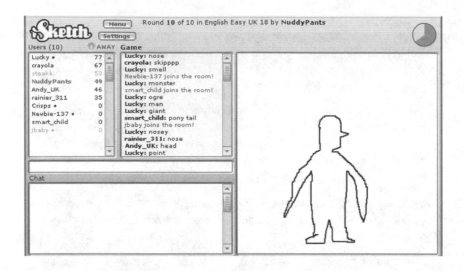

Figure 6.1 *iSketch* Provides an Example of Multiple Simultaneous Players (image reproduced with permission of iSketch.net)

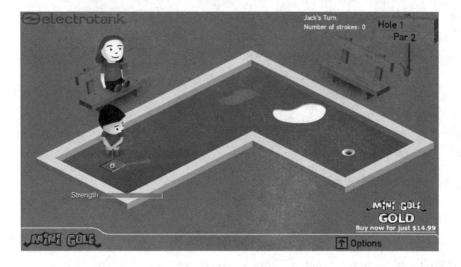

Figure 6.2 *Mini Golf* Allows Two Players to Play Together (image reproduced with permission of Electrotank, Inc.)

number of players per instance of the game (in case the total present was not exactly divisible by that number). The solution I used was to make the game playable by either three or four players (with the fourth player optional and playing a mediation role). In practice, because of students turning up late, there were often players left over after all the games had started, in which case latecomers were asked to work with one of the players already taking part, using a combination of methods to ensure collaboration.

Activities to Support Learning with Games

As well as collaboration, I feel that briefing and reflection are two essential activities for ensuring that students understand the purpose of the game and relate the activities that have taken place during the game to the intended learning outcomes from playing it. In terms of the learning package that surrounds an educational game, debriefing, post-game discussion and reflection are regarded by some as a key aspect to ensuring that the learning is focused and appropriate (e.g. Bredemeir & Greenblat, 1981; Thiagarajan, 1993). In fact, Thiagarajan and Jasinski, more recently, go as far as to say:

> The game is an excuse for the debrief... debriefing provides the opportunity for reflection to take place which hopefully will facilitate the transfer of learning from the game to the work context.
>
> (Thiagarajan and Jasinski, 2004, online)

Debriefing and reflection on learning is not a typical component of computer games designed solely for entertainment, and is also an aspect that is frequently not given due consideration in relation to the design of educational computer games. Kolb's (1984) experiential learning cycle describes learning activities as a sequence of phases of experience, observation and reflection, creating abstract theories from the experience, and testing in new situations. While I would argue that games are excellent vehicles for providing experiences and application of theories, I think that they are less well able to provide meaningful reflection and abstract conceptualization. Additional learning activities that surround the game are an excellent opportunity for stimulating reflection on the game, which is often not an intrinsic part of the game itself. Without adequate briefing, students may not understand the purpose of the game, what they are supposed to do, or what the point is, and therefore may not be appropriately engaged. Debriefing and reflective activities after and during the game support consolidation of learning from the game, its application to the real world and the transferability of learning to other contexts. There are a variety of ways in which additional activities can be built into game play, and some examples are provided in the box.

By seeing the whole gaming experience as a mixture of in-game and out-of-game activities, there is a far greater opportunity for meeting all of the required learning outcomes, transferring knowledge and skills to other contexts, supporting theorizing and generalization, and facilitating other transferable skills such as writing, evaluation and presentation skills. In my opinion, the

Reflective accounts, diaries or logs that students keep of their progress through the game, considering what is happening at a given point, justifying decisions taken, and reflecting on the gaming process as well as the outcomes.

Small group work where students discuss what has happened during the game, the implications of decisions taken and what could have happened differently. Asking students to consider specific aspects of the processes that happened during the game (e.g. collaboration, problem-solving, negotiation) and think about how they could have been done differently or better.

Replaying the game, or aspects of it, and talking through the thought processes involved and how performance could be or has improved in light of what has been learned. Development of *what-if* scenarios that consider what could have happened under different circumstances.

Production of artefacts that relate to the game, such as posters, presentations, graphics or rich media.

Storytelling or other creative activities around the characters or plot of the game, getting students to think about what happened next in the narrative.

Application of skills to the real world through activities that build on skills acquired during the game. For example, using problem-solving skills developed in an adventure play and applying them to solve similar real-world problems.

Critique of the game itself and its mechanics, considering how it worked, how effective it was, how much it related to the real world and how it could be improved.

activities that surround the game are crucial for developing a complete learning package.

The way in which assessment is integrated into an educational game is also a good opportunity to stimulate student reflection. For example, the use of reflective diaries while playing a game, portfolios based on artefacts created in the game or reports justifying decisions taken during the game can form part of the overall assessment for a course of study. While I feel that it is important that students are not directly assessed on their performance in a game, a variety of creative assessment activities can be used to supplement the effectiveness of the game and support reflection (this is covered in greater detail in Chapter 7).

Designing Digital Games for Learning

There are several different options available to educators for obtaining, or creating, a desired game. In this section I briefly explore some of these options before looking at some guidance on what makes an effective educational game and how to develop a game specification before you start.

Unfortunately, the average lecturer is unlikely to have access to the many millions of pounds required to create a bespoke commercial quality game. However, there are various ways to go about obtaining games for learning and here I will provide a brief overview of the main options (these are discussed in greater detail in Chapters 8 and 9).

Using a Commercial Entertainment Game

This approach has the advantage of enabling students to use a high-end product, which has been explicitly designed to be fun and engaging. However, many commercial games are also expensive and it can be difficult to find a game that exactly matches the desired learning outcomes.

Modifying Existing Games

Some gaming environments now come with an additional creation engine that allows the development of extensions to the game such as new storylines or areas (known as 'modding').

Using Commercial Educational Games

Commercial gaming environments do exist that are specifically designed for learning. These can still be expensive, and are often difficult to customize if they do not meet the exact requirements of the learners or curriculum.

Using Virtual Worlds

The use of multi-user virtual environments (MUVEs) such as *Second Life* for learning has increased greatly in recent years. Although many people would argue that these worlds are not technically games, I include them here because of their potential to create interactive and explorative environments.

Creating Bespoke Games

This has the major advantage of being able to design a game where the learning outcomes are closely aligned with gaming outcomes for a specific curriculum and student group. While some technical expertise is required, there are a growing number of development tools available for game creation.

Learners as Game Creators

Instead of students being viewed as players of games (or merely consumers of content) they can learn by developing or creating games themselves. The easy availability of game development tools and modification engines makes this a more feasible option, but still some level of technical and design expertise is required by students.

Although there are a number of options for producing digital games for learning, as presented in this section, it is unlikely in the context of higher education, with limited budgets and development expertise available, that it will ever be possible to obtain the perfect game for a given teaching situation. Essentially, I feel that the use of digital games for learning will have to be undertaken with a high degree of pragmatism, and this again highlights the importance of not seeing a game as a stand-alone activity but as part of a learning package of activities.

When deciding what types of game would be appropriate in any given context there are a number of factors that must be considered. Whether a game is useful and appropriate will depend on the type of students and their backgrounds, experiences and preferences, coupled with the nature of the discipline, curriculum and learning outcomes, and the expertise of the teacher, or development team. These factors will determine what is most appropriate in any given situation.

Once you have some idea of the approach you would like to take to obtaining your desired game, I always think it is a good idea to write a short design specification, which you can use as a starting point for developing or finding the game you need. At the end of this chapter I provide an example of a specification and there is an activity in which you can create your own, but before then I want to look briefly at what is good practice in effective game design for learning, as this will help you think about ways of addressing different aspects of the game specification.

Effective Game Design for Learning

In this subsection I look at some of the findings from my own research into ways to support the effective design of games for learning. First I introduce a set of criteria, which are designed to be used to support the development of games for learning or evaluate the potential of particular games for use with students in higher education. These criteria present a framework for good practice in design from an active learning perspective, but are not intended to be prescriptive, and there may well be examples of excellent educational games that do not adhere to one or more of these recommendations. These guidelines were developed from a review and synthesis of existing learning design guidelines coupled with an analysis of existing popular entertainment games.

- The environment should *support active learning* by encouraging exploration, problem-solving and enquiry, providing opportunities for students to test ideas and gain feedback, practice and consolidate their learning. Opportunities for collaboration should also be provided and, as much as possible, game goals should align with learning outcomes.
- The environment should *engender engagement*, with explicit and achievable goals, provision of a large world to be explored with a high level of interactivity, multiple pathways and different ways in which success can be achieved. The world should stimulate the user's curiosity and provide an appropriate level of challenge and control of the environment.
- The gaming world should be *appropriate for the learning context*, in that it fits with, or is at least relevant to, curriculum and assessment, is suitable for the subject area, matches the time available, and is personally relevant to and acceptable by the students who use it.
- The environment or associated activities should support and provide *opportunities for reflection*, allow students to debrief from the game and contextualize their learning, and highlight the process of learning.
- The environment must provide an equitable *experience* for all users, taking into account and accommodating differing prior knowledge and experience of that gaming world and similar environments. Ideally it should allow for personalization and customization and provide equal opportunities for all students to participate. Where possible, alternative pedagogic approaches should be available to students, aligned to their personal learning preferences.
- The gaming world needs to provide *ongoing support*, from initial orientation to early tasks that provide quick initial success, with a gradual introduction of increasing complexity, supported with help, hints or clues to ensure that the environment does not become limiting. The gaming experience should aim to extend players to their extreme level of competence.

Implicit in these guidelines is the assumption that collaborative learning is a prerequisite of *all* learning, and I recognize that this is certainly not the case for all aspects of learning in higher education as plenty of examples exist of excellent individual learning. What I have tried to do by adding it as a guideline here is to ensure that the potential for collaboration is considered (even if you then decide that it is not appropriate). Additionally, learning by rote or didactic approaches can be effective in complex skill and competency development, and examples exist in the medical and engineering disciplines. However, I would argue that computer games provide an excellent forum for stimulating collaborative learning at a higher level and that working with others has a great potential for creating effective learning experiences.

The guidelines also make the assumption that reflection is a requirement of all higher education learning activities, which is clearly also not always the case. I feel, however, that it is important to highlight the reflective aspects, as this is an area that is often neglected in computer game-based learning.

The creation of complex interactive worlds also assumes a level of competence in the course designer to develop 'engaging' immersive content and activities in the gaming medium, which may not always be feasible. However the 'interactive world' does not end with the use of the computer and there is always the potential to design for interaction in the real world.

While these guidelines were developed from a constructivist standpoint, I do recognize that games can also be used effectively as instructional tools in adult learning contexts in further and higher education, adult and community learning, the corporate training sector and in military applications For example, the most widely accessed serious game is the America's Army recruitment game with over 17 million downloads (although, interestingly, some users are now subverting the use of this game to create an environment for self-expression and forum for anti-war protest). However, my real interest, and where I see the real potential in higher education, is in viewing games as constructivist learning environments.

Developing a Game Concept Specification

Whenever I start thinking about using a new game for learning, I find that completing a game concept specification early on is very helpful. It allows me to collect all my thoughts and ideas in one place and start to clarify exactly what it is I intend to use. A document like this is also really useful if you are working with others and need to communicate your ideas. Table 6.2 shows the concept specification for the *Time Capsule* game.

The aim of the concept specification is really just to get some of your initial ideas on paper and to clarify some of your thinking. It will also act as the basis for the more detailed functional specification that you will need to create if you are thinking about creating the game for yourself. The concept specification gets you to think about what type of game you might want to create, what genre it might belong to, the narrative context and the types of activities that players will undertake during the game. I also find it useful early on to describe the ways in which collaboration and reflection might be facilitated in the game and the activities that surround it.

At this stage, some of your ideas can still be fairly vague; there will be plenty of time to tighten them up later when you come to actually find or create the game you need. At this stage you should really view the concept specification as a way of gathering your thoughts and looking at possibilities.

The purpose of the concept specification is really to get your ideas on paper and to help you think through some of the issues that might exist. Don't worry

Table 6.2 Concept Specification for *The Time Capsule*

Learning objectives	Be able to communicate successfully with others. Be able to successfully work together and reach effective decisions. Be aware of the elements that make a group effective.
Genre	Multi-player strategy / negotiation game.
Brief description	Multi-player online game in which players have to adopt the role of a character and negotiate with other players regarding items to be included in a time capsule.
Plot	Four local dignitaries have to select six items to be included in a time capsule to represent the local town. Each character has different objectives and preferences.
Gaming activities	Communication with other players regarding personal needs. Making a decision as a group that all parties agree on. The number of items will be limited and each item will have a cost. The group will have to agree on the items and keep within budget.
Constraints	Game will take a maximum of 45 minutes to run. Game will be played on a single occasion. Game will be played in a computer lab.
Collaboration	Players will play in small groups online but in the same physical space.
Reflection	Players will undertake a reflective activity at the end of the game. Players can review the conversation that has taken place during the game.

if at this stage your ideas are still vague – the game design process is very much an iterative one, and you could find it very useful at this stage to run your ideas past a colleague to take advantage of a fresh perspective.

I hope that after reading this chapter you will now have a good idea of how to go about the first steps in designing a game for learning, and realize that this design and initial specification process is still useful even if you intend to use a commercial game rather than create one for yourself, because it will help to ensure that the game you end up with is really the one you need. We will take the next step of finding or developing a game for yourself in Chapters 8 and 9 below. However, in the next chapter I will look at different ways in which you can assess the learning that has taken place during a game.

Activity: Specifying a Game Concept

If you haven't yet completed the contextual analysis activity in the previous chapter and the learning objectives mapping activity in this chapter, I suggest you do so before undertaking this activity.

Using the questions from the example game concept specification shown above, take some time now to think about how you might go about specifying a concept for a game that you could use in your own context.

You will find the contextual analysis and mapping to be a useful starting point to help you think about what you want to achieve and the limitations that exist.

Chapter Summary

This chapter focused on aspects of designing a game for learning, looking first at pedagogic design considerations, including the importance of aligning learning objectives with game activities, ways of supporting collaboration and activities that support reflection and learning from games.

In the second section I briefly talked about six options for obtaining appropriate games for learning: commercial entertainment games; modifying entertainment games; commercial educational games; virtual worlds; bespoke games; and students as game creators.

I then presented six guidelines for the design of effective games for learning:

- support for active learning;
- engendering engagement;
- appropriateness for the learning context;
- opportunities for reflection;
- equitable experience;
- ongoing support.

The chapter finished with an example of a design concept specification.

CHAPTER 7

Assessing the Impact of Digital Games on Learning

In this chapter I discuss issues associated with assessing the impact of digital games on learning from two different angles. The first section looks at how games can be formally assessed and appropriate ways to undertake assessment. The second section looks at ways in which the impact on learning can be researched and assessed.

Whether the use of games forms part of the formal assessment for a course and the way in which it is implemented can heavily influence the way in which students engage with the game and their learning from it. The first section of this chapter looks at the different ways that exist of assessing learning with digital games, and considers their implications.

In addition to being a means of evaluating students' progress, carrying out assessment is also useful in order to determine whether employing a digital game for learning has been successful. Given that this is still a relatively new, and unproven, teaching method in higher education, I feel it is important to carry out research activities around the use of digital games. The research evidence that exists as to the effectiveness of digital games is limited, so the gathering of data to support (or otherwise) their employment is useful to the research and practitioner community as a whole, as well as to inform your own teaching practice and lead to improvements in subsequent iterations of use of any specific game.

In the second section of this chapter I discuss the rationale for carrying out research in digital games for learning before going on to discuss ways of evaluating learning and engagement. The final section highlights some ethical issues associated with carrying out research of this type.

Assessment of Learning from Digital Games

Whether, and how, a game is assessed will influence how students engage with it. Students are notoriously assessment-centred and using game play as part of the formative or summative assessment for a course is one way to ensure that students engage with it. However, designing appropriate assessment activities that complement the learning undertaken in a game is not always straightforward. The concept of alignment between learning objectives, gaming activities and assessment activities is again important here.

Deciding to assess a particular game or not may depend on a number of factors such as the importance of the game in the course overall and the scope for changing the assessment (while it is often quite straightforward at universities to modify learning activities, altering assessments can require a time-consuming engagement with the institution's Quality Enhancement procedures). If using a game itself is an innovation, you may feel uncomfortable also making an innovation in assessment, but it is important that the type of assessment is appropriate for the activities undertaken and the desired learning. For example, if students have spent the whole course being actively engaged in a game that has developed their critical thinking and analytical skills then a multiple-choice test that requires memorization of facts would not be appropriate.

The way in which any game is assessed is crucial if it is to be purposeful, to be seen as appropriate by the students and to encourage them to engage in the learning experience. I think that it is very important not to relate performance in the game to performance in the overall assessment. There are two reasons for this, first because a poor performance in the game does not necessarily mean that a student is not learning from it. The ability to make mistakes in a safe environment and learn from them is one of the key benefits of game-based learning and to directly relate performance to assessment would negate this. Secondly, it could also be the case that poor performance in the game has been due to other factors such as inability to navigate in a virtual world or lack of experience with the game genre. In this case, players who had more experience playing games would be at an unfair advantage over those with less experience.

The way in which an overall course assessment relates to a game will, of course, depend on the prominence of the game in the course overall. If it is played on one occasion then the impact on, and relation to, the overall assessment will be less than if the entire course is based around a game. Learning with games can be assessed in the usual wide variety of ways available in higher education, but if assessment can be linked into the game itself it will be contextualized and taking part in the game will be more meaningful and purposeful. There are some examples below of the ways in which assessments can be incorporated into the use of a digital game:

- Reports on actions taken and decisions made, with critical analysis of the consequences of decisions, or on future planning based on the endpoint of the game.
- Presentations on aspects of a game using roles from within the game (e.g. in a business game this could involve making a group presentation to the board of directors explaining the rationale for decisions taken).
- Creation of artefacts based on and extending the action in the game (e.g. posters, digital video, audio, graphics).
- Discussion posts can be assessed for their contribution, critical engagement with and reflection on the game.
- Collaborative websites, using tools such as blogs or wikis can be used to encourage students to work together to create an ongoing log of actions taken and learning from the game.
- Narratives associated with the action in the game (e.g. characterizations, back stories, future scenarios).
- Reflective accounts of the actions taken in the game and the learning acquired from it.
- Portfolios detailing the use of the game, decisions made, artefacts created, consequences and learning.

Designing appropriate assessment for game-based learning is an opportunity to be creative and develop the skills learned in the game as applied to the real world. Thought needs to be put into ensuring that the type of assessment is appropriate for the type of active learning that takes place in games, so that it is part of the overall learning experience and not merely a way of measuring learning. Examples of ways in which game-based courses can be assessed in practice are provided in Case Studies 2, 3 and 5.

I am very much of the view that assessment should be seen as a learning activity itself and not simply as a measurement activity; this ensures that it can be used to enhance the overall game-based experience. Integrating a number of small formative assessments during the course of the game is a good way to ensure sustained engagement and to provide students with ongoing feedback, highlight mistakes and misconceptions early and give ongoing support and encouragement.

It may well be the case, depending on university quality procedures and whether you have the luxury of designing a game-based course from scratch, that you have little opportunity to change the ways in which a given course is formally assessed in the short term. However, there may still be opportunities

Activity: Designing an Assessment Activity

If you have not completed the first activity in Chapter 6 on aligning game activities and learning objectives, I suggest you complete it before undertaking this activity.

For each of the objectives listed in your mapping consider whether it is currently assessed. If it is, write down the method.

If these activities are already assessed are the methods appropriate for your game?

Can you think of any better ways in which the assessment could be integrated within the game play?

for integrating formative assessment in the process (although it may be difficult to ensure that students engage if the assessments do not contribute to their overall final marks).

Researching Learning with Digital Games

Here I look at ways in which learning with digital games can be assessed for the purposes of research. I talk first about the importance of carrying out research into all types of educational innovation, game-based or otherwise, because of the need to try to assess the impact of any change or intervention. Digital game-based learning in particular raises issues of acceptability and appropriateness in the context of higher education, so it is of prime importance that practitioners can justify what they are doing and provide evidence that the innovation has been successful. There is still limited evidence as to the effectiveness of the approach – not because it is not a valid method of enhancing teaching and learning but simply because there is a lack of robust research evidence in the field (de Freitas, 2007).

There are two reasons why I feel it is really important to evaluate the use of digital games for learning in higher education. First, research evaluation can be used to show the impact of a novel method of teaching in a range of areas, including learning and student progress, application of learning to the real world, the student experience and motivation. Without evaluation it is impossible to tell whether the game has been successful, or provide evidence of its effectiveness. Secondly, research into the effectiveness of any games you use will enable you to identify areas of the game-based learning package that worked well, and those that were less successful, in order to be able to modify and improve its use in future.

Connolly and colleagues (2008) present a framework for the evaluation of game-based learning, based on a comprehensive literature review of the area.

They propose that there are seven aspects that should be examined when determining the effectiveness of game-based learning.

- *Learner performance* – whether learning has taken place and there is an improvement in learner performance.
- *Motivation* – the levels of student motivation, interest and participation in the game.
- *Perceptions* – the views of the students towards areas such as the experience of time passing, the realism of the game, amounts of complexity, support received and levels of perceived proficiency within the game.
- *Attitudes* – feelings of the learners and teachers towards the subject itself and the use of games for learning within that subject.
- *Collaboration* – the regularity and effectiveness of collaboration. (Connolly *et al.* argue that this is optional and dependent on the game design; I would argue that in the context of adult learning with games collaboration is an important part of the learning design.)
- *Preferences* – inclinations of the learners and teachers towards, for example, different learning styles or modes of interaction.
- *Game-Based Learning Environment* – factors associated with the game itself, such as the design of the environment, use of scaffolding, usability, levels of social presence and the way in which the game is deployed.

This framework provides an excellent overview of the types of elements that could be researched in respect to the effectiveness of game-based learning. In the rest of this chapter I consider ways in which the first six items on this list can be researched. Issues associated with the game-based learning environment itself are discussed in Chapter 10. Here, I look first at researching learning (or learner performance) and secondly at ways in which to research the student experience (looking at issues such as motivation, perceptions, attitudes, collaboration and preferences).

Researching Learning

A common way of measuring learning from a unit of study is through the assessment for that unit. However, this is often not possible in the case of much game-based learning simply because the learning from the game isn't directly assessed or because the learning from the game forms a small part of a much larger overall set of learning objectives. If a computer game is only being used in one or two classes or as a small proportion of the course as a whole, then it may not have a large enough impact on the overall course assessment to be evaluated in this way.

In the case of a larger game-based intervention, where the game is embedded within the course, an analysis of assessment scores is a potential way in which to evaluate learning. However, without a basis for comparison it is difficult to say whether the game has actually made a difference to learning. This can be obtained for example by comparing the overall grades from one year to the next or between two groups using different teaching methods, but assumes that the game and alternative (traditional) way of teaching the learning objectives are equivalent and are comparable over time. In any case of teaching two different groups using different methods there are also ethical issues that arise in ensuring that each of the groups has a comparable experience (these will be discussed later in the chapter).

There are also different types of learning (or unintended learning objectives) that you are interested in researching but may not be adequately represented in the assessment, such as the long-term retention of learning or the ability to appropriately apply the learning in real-life contexts. Valuable transferable skills, such as problem-solving, teamwork or negotiation, may also have been learned during a game-based learning experience which were not intended learning objectives but of value nonetheless, and these may not be reflected in the assessment.

In experimental design studies, the effectiveness of an educational innovation is often measured using a test before the game (pre-test), followed by the intervention, followed by a second equivalent test (post-test). Differences in the pre- and post-test scores can indicate that the intervention has caused increased learning (or in the case of comparative studies different levels of learning in the target group compared to the control group). This technique has been used for a number of studies on game-based learning; for example, Ebner and Holzinger (2006) tested theoretical knowledge in chemical engineering, Kambouri *et al.* (2006) evaluated basic literacy skills, and Sung et al. (2008) examined children's understanding of taxonomic concepts. However, there are a number of potential problems with this approach: if the learning objectives are knowledge-based and involve the memorization of facts then they may be easy to evaluate with something like a simple test, but I would argue that the best use of games in higher education is not to focus on these lower level learning outcomes but on higher level outcomes that involve synthesis, evaluation and critical thinking – outcomes that are not so straightforward or quick to test. There is also the issue of equivalence between the two tests (which cannot be identical because it would then be impossible to distinguish between learning from the game and learning from having previously completed the same test) and how you can ensure that they are of the same difficulty and assess exactly the same aspects of learning.

Another issue with the pre-test/post-test model for the higher level learning outcomes and affective skills that games can be used to teach is that, while it would be possible to design a pre- and post-test for these type of skills, it would involve undertaking comparable tasks. This in itself could bias the results by acting as a learning as well as an evaluative activity, and would be time-consuming and impractical to administer. It may also be difficult, if not impossible, to persuade students to give up extra time for this type of testing. Difficulties with getting students to cooperate with the pre-/post-test model because of the extra work required on their part are not uncommon. Squire (2005), for example, could not persuade the students in his sample group to complete a pre-test at all. The timing of the post-test also has to be carefully designed so account for retention of learning over time and application of learning to other contexts, and again it may be difficult to persuade the same students to take part after some period of time, particularly when their participation will happen too late to influence the design of their own courses.

Another way of researching learning is by using student self-evaluation. While the data gathered from such an exercise may not be robust – self-evaluation of this type is notoriously inaccurate – it does at least allow the ability to gather some data as to whether students think they have learned something from taking part in game-based learning. When I have used self-evaluation of this type I have added control questions that relate to other learning outcomes, not intended to be met by the particular game-based activity, as a means of evaluating the way in which students were completing their forms and to increase the validity of the results.

Other ways of evaluating learning with games include analysis of communication transcripts (e.g. to highlight evidence of critical thinking, lateral thinking, collaboration, etc.) and a range of quantitative measures (e.g. time spent playing the game, points accrued, levels reached and so on). There are many difficulties associated with evaluation of learning in higher education, particularly when higher level cognitive skills are being evaluated. Carefully designed, constructively aligned, assessments are essential but can only provide evidence of learning from a game if it is an integral part of a course. Quantitative measures, such as assessment scores, do not on their own provide the whole picture and it is important also to use qualitative methods (such as interviews) to find out more about the student experience of learning with games.

Assessing the Student Experience

As well as evaluating learning from games, there are other aspects of the student experience that can be evaluated and relate to learning, including student motivations, attitudes to and perceptions of the game, their preferences and experience of collaboration. You can look at questions such as how much students enjoyed using the game, for example, whether they felt it was preferable to other learning methods, whether they felt that they were more actively engaged than with other learning activities.

There are a variety of methods for gathering data on these aspects of the student experience, including questionnaires, attitudinal scales, interviews, focus groups, and observation. Details of these techniques can be found in any introductory book on research in education or the social sciences, so I will not go into a great deal of detail here. However, whether students enjoyed using a particular way to learn does not necessarily relate to how effective that method is for actually learning something.

An approach that I favour in terms of understanding the student experience (and gaining an indication of learning) is to look at student engagement with the game. Measuring engagement with a game-based learning experience is one way of gaining an insight into how effective it was for learning, as higher levels of engagement with a learning activity are indicative of increased learning from it. Jacques et al. (1995) argue that designing interactions to be engaging can encourage and facilitate learning, and Lepper and Malone (1987) provide evidence that there is a link between intrinsic motivation to learn, engagement and instructional effectiveness. It is important, however, to distinguish between engagement with a game, and engagement with the intended learning from the game. Ideally, educational games should be designed so that the game outcomes are aligned with the learning outcomes so that engagement in the game supports learning.

The most common methods employed to measure engagement in educational settings are the use of questionnaires and measurements such as time-on-task or attendance rates (e.g. Chapman, 2003). Other techniques include analysis of facial expressions and body language (Hughey, 2002), observations (Read et al., 2002) and voluntary time on task (Virvou et al., 2004). I have developed a questionnaire that allows me to measure levels of engagement with a particular learning experience by asking students about their perceptions of that experience. This questionnaire is intended to be used to compare two learning experiences rather than provide an absolute measure of engagement. I developed and tested an attitudinal scale to measure post-experiential engagement with educational games; this may be a useful tool for others interested in a more quantitative way of evaluating the student experience.

In order to create this scale, I first identified the factors that I thought might contribute to the concept of engagement with learning. In determining these factors, flow theory (Csikszentmihalyi, 1992) was used as a central basis, but hypothesizing that flow is actually an extreme form of engagement and that it is possible to be engaged while not actually in a state of flow. I also drew on the work of Malone (1980), in terms of challenge, curiosity and control and took into consideration adult learning theory regarding adults' motivations for learning (Knowles, 1998), which argues that adults need to know why they should learn something before they are willing to invest time and energy in learning it, and become ready to learn something when they need to apply it to be able to cope effectively with real-life situations. In addition to these theories, the results from my own interviews, described earlier in this book, contributed to this model of adult engagement with game-based learning, which is postulated to be made up of five separate factors.

- *Perception of challenge* – the motivation to undertake the activity, clarity as to what it involves and a perception that the task is achievable but not trivial.
- *Perception of control* – the fairness of the activity, the level of choice over types of action that can be taken in the environment and the speed and transparency of feedback.
- *Immersion* – the extent to which the individual is absorbed in the activity.
- *Interest* – the intrinsic interest of the individual in the activity or its subject matter.
- *Purpose* – the perceived value of the activity for learning, whether it is seen as being worthwhile in the context of study.

For the most part, these factors are clearly linked to prior research in the arena of games and engagement. However, it is worth highlighting the factor of purpose, which would not necessarily contribute to engagement with a purely entertainment activity. A clear finding from the interviews I conducted was that the adult learners were highly strategic in their learning, wanted to learn in the most effective manner possible and were unlikely to be motivated by a learning activity simply because it was a game; the purpose of a game for learning seemed to have a clear impact on the levels of engagement with it. The questionnaire developed is shown in Table 7.1.

This questionnaire can be used after an activity has been completed to evaluate the level of engagement relative to another activity. In order to analyse the results and compare levels of engagement between two different activities the following steps should be taken.

- Allocate a value to each answer, where strongly disagree = 1 to strongly agree = 5 (as this is a relative scale rather than an absolute value you could equally well allocate values from strongly disagree = −2 to strongly agree = 2).
- For negative items (e.g. 'I could not tell what effect my actions had') reverse this scale.
- Add up the total points to get a value for engagement with the activity.

Table 7.1 Engagement Questionnaire

Thinking about the activity you have just undertaken, please indicate the level to which you agree with the following statements:

	Strongly disagree	Disagree	Neither agree nor disagree	Agree	Strongly agree
I wanted to complete the activity	☐	☐	☐	☐	☐
I found the activity frustrating	☐	☐	☐	☐	☐
I felt that I could achieve the goal of the activity	☐	☐	☐	☐	☐
I knew what I had to do to complete the activity	☐	☐	☐	☐	☐
I found the activity boring	☐	☐	☐	☐	☐
It wasn't clear what I could and couldn't do	☐	☐	☐	☐	☐
It was clear what I could learn from the activity	☐	☐	☐	☐	☐
I felt absorbed in the activity	☐	☐	☐	☐	☐
The activity was pointless	☐	☐	☐	☐	☐
I was not interested in exploring the options available	☐	☐	☐	☐	☐
I did not care how the activity ended	☐	☐	☐	☐	☐
I felt that time passed quickly	☐	☐	☐	☐	☐
I found the activity satisfying	☐	☐	☐	☐	☐
The activity would not let me do what I wanted	☐	☐	☐	☐	☐
I could not tell what effect my actions had	☐	☐	☐	☐	☐
I did not enjoy the activity	☐	☐	☐	☐	☐
Feedback I was given was useful	☐	☐	☐	☐	☐
I found it easy to get started	☐	☐	☐	☐	☐

You can then compare relative engagement scores for different activities or for different people. If you want to test whether this is statistically significant you should use an appropriate non-parametric test, in this instance I would suggest a Mann–Whitney test. (I won't go into the statistical details here but leave you to carry out this research yourself if you are interested. You will be able to find details in most introductory books on statistics for research.)

Activity: Comparing Your Engagement During Different Activities

Select your favourite and least preferred game from the examples described in the introductory chapter of this book (or other games if you prefer).

Play each of these games for 20 minutes, and after playing each game complete the questionnaire above about your experience (complete the questionnaire directly after playing each game).

Do you think you were more engaged in one game than the other?

Calculate your engagement scores for each of these games. Is there a difference?

By completing this activity you will hopefully see how the questionnaire can be used to measure engagement between two activities, as well as realizing that different activities will engage different people at different times. I am not suggesting that this measure of engagement should replace qualitative data collection and analysis methods (such as interviews or focus groups) as a way of assessing the impact of a game for learning, but that it provides an additional quantitative method.

Ethics of Researching Learning

To finish off this chapter, I want to look briefly at some of the ethical issues that arise when undertaking any research in education. In any form of evaluative or research activity it is important to consider the ethical implications and so it is worth taking a few minutes here to consider some of the ethical issues associated with evaluating game-based learning in particular, and any learning intervention in general.

It is crucial that all participants in the research have given voluntary and informed consent to take part. It is the right of any participant in research to take part knowingly and not to be deceived or have information misrepresented about any aspects of the research (although very occasionally a level of deception might be necessary for the research). Therefore, while students may not have the right to 'opt out' of the game-based learning experience itself if it is part of the standard learning activities of the course, they should always have the right not to take part in any associated evaluative activity if they wish not to. Students also have the right not to be coerced, stressed or placed under discomfort; although this should be obvious it is possible, for example, to give the impression that not taking part in an evaluation will be looked poorly upon and may affect course marks.

Ensuring the privacy of participants is crucial. It is important that you have considered how you want to deal with the issues of anonymity, confidentiality and data security and that students are aware of these issues before they agree to take part in the research. This may manifest itself when you come to consider how you will make use of the findings; again, it is crucial to know what you plan to do with the data that you collect and that this is communicated to the students. For example, it would be unethical to collect feedback in the form of questionnaires for evaluative purposes and then use quotes as part of marketing materials without the explicit consent of the students who had provided the quotes.

Enthusing students to take part in evaluative and research activities is one of the hardest areas that I have encountered in my own research. In some cases, particularly if your evaluation is lengthy or time-consuming, you may want to pay students to take part or provide some other sort of incentive. There is nothing unethical about this in itself but it is important to make sure that access to the option of taking part is equitable and that the fact that students are being paid does not bias your findings.

In the case of comparative studies (i.e. where you are evaluating differences between students in two or more different conditions) it is important that at no point is taking part in this research detrimental to participants. This is particularly relevant when alternative experimental conditions are used as a required part of a programme of study, for example when some students are taught in a traditional manner and some use game-based learning. If you think that one way is better than another then you are implicitly putting those students in the other condition at a disadvantage. Giving students choices about what method they prefer can address the ethical issues but then may mean that the research design is invalid.

This is the final chapter in the part of the book devoted to the practical issues associated with the use of game-based learning in higher education. In the next part, which focuses on technology, I will examine some of the different ways of obtaining or producing digital games, and look at the range of technical considerations that arise.

Chapter Summary

This chapter has looked at a number of ways to assess learning that has taken place in digital games, both from the point of view of formal assessment and in undertaking research into the effectiveness of games.

A rationale for using engagement as a way of assessing the student experience was provided, and a questionnaire for evaluating engagement with game-based learning presented, based around five factors: perception of challenge, perception of control, immersion, interest and purpose.

Finally, ethical issues were highlighted and discussed around voluntary informed consent, privacy, participant rights, use of data, payment and comparative studies.

Further Reading

M. Densombe (2002). *Ground Rules for Good Research: A 10 Point Guide for Social Researchers*. Maidenhead: Open University Press. Excellent and accessible for anyone wanting to carry out research into teaching and learning.

C. Robson (2002). *Real World Research*. Malden, MA: Blackwell. I highly recommend this as an introduction to research.

CHAPTER 8

Using Existing Digital Games for Learning

In this chapter I discuss a variety of ways in which commercial games and virtual worlds can be used to support teaching and learning in higher education. I examine the differences between games designed for entertainment and education and look at the advantages and disadvantages of the different options available to educators. Finally, I provide details of a number of websites where you can start to look for existing games that you might find useful in your teaching.

Throughout, I have tried to provide examples of the different ways in which existing digital games can be used to enhance learning in higher education. Unfortunately, there are few examples of the effective use of existing games in this context, so I draw on examples from the school sector, and highlight principles behind the use of the games that could be transferred to the higher education domain. I hope that after reading this chapter you will have an overview of the ways in which commercial games can be used or adapted and have a feeling about whether this approach would be useful for you.

Once you have decided that you want to use a digital game to support teaching and learning (and have decided not to opt for creating a game from scratch) finding the right game can be a big challenge. In the first section I examine the rationale for using existing digital games – both those designed for entertainment and those explicitly designed for learning – in higher education. There are many advantages to using existing games over bespoke games: commercial games have already had a great deal of money spent on their production, ensuring that they are of sound technical quality and high in playability; they are designed to be fun and engaging; they have high production values and look professional.

However, there are also a number of drawbacks to using existing games in that they can be expensive, may take a long time to learn how to play, require computers with high-end specifications, can contain inappropriate or distracting content, and take a long time to complete (both for the students and for a teacher during evaluation). In addition, games designed for entertainment may be perceived as time-wasting by some students precisely because of their high production values and the fact that they are obviously games designed for entertainment. An important challenge with the use of existing games is ensuring the match between the intended learning objectives and the gaming activities, which may require the development of carefully considered activities to support the use of the game.

Differences between Games for Entertainment and Learning

When considering whether to use an existing game for learning it is important to understand the differences in how digital games are designed for entertainment compared to those specifically designed for learning. This section explores some of these differences in more detail, and discusses the design implications when developing a learning package based around an existing entertainment game.

I think it is worth pointing out at this stage that this analysis again takes an active learning perspective, focusing on learning that involves problem-solving, creation of context, experiential learning, and usually collaboration, and that the advice in the chapter relates directly to higher level learning outcomes around critical thinking, synthesis, analysis and application. Although I accept that other paradigms of learning do exist, the focus of this book is viewing games as active learning environments rather than tools to aid recall. Many of the educational games that exist in the sphere of children's learning – and are often referred to as edutainment – are based around extrinsic rewards (e.g. answer some maths questions and get rewarded by some game play) and drill-and-practice; while this might be appropriate for some situations and groups this is not the focus of the educational design presented here.

Educational games can differ from entertainment games in a number of ways. For example, there are likely to be differences in fidelity and graphical quality and the way in which the game is implemented (e.g. the platform it runs on), purpose of the game and the types of activity it involves, the way that the game itself is learned, the time taken to play the game, and the way that collaboration and competition are integrated into the game design. In the subsections that follow I explore these issues in greater detail.

Fidelity and Graphical Quality

Commercial entertainment games have massively high budgets in comparison to games that are designed for education. In the context of higher education, games – even those designed for introductory areas with applicability to large student groups – have much less mass-market appeal than, for example, games aimed at school-level students where there is a standard country-wide curriculum. Given these conditions, there is no way that educational games can hope to compete with entertainment games in terms of the creation of high-fidelity virtual gaming worlds. There is some disagreement within the community of educational game researchers over whether the level of fidelity and graphical quality of the gaming environment is crucial in terms of playability and learning. It has been argued that entertainment games with higher production values are more popular and sell more copies than those with lower production values, and therefore are more motivational and engaging, and that the greater level of realism in high-end games leads to a greater sense of immersion. However, I would argue that in the context of higher education, commercial high-end production values are not necessary to produce a valuable and effective learning experience – it is the design of the game itself that far more greatly affects the levels of immersion and engagement.

In fact, high-end games with complex interfaces may even be offputting to some learners, particularly those who are not used to playing this type of game, because of the steep learning curve required to navigate the interface and learn how to play the game itself. Some learners may also find this type of game less acceptable in the higher education context. I personally think that as long as the game production values are not so poor as to actually detract from the learning or give an impression of amateurishness (e.g. with a poorly designed user interface or system that is not robust) then the level of graphical quality is somewhat irrelevant.

There is also debate within the research community about the level of realism that is required in games for them to be effective. While realism can lead to greater immersion, it can also detract from the learning process in educational games, making transfer of learning to other situations in the real world more difficult. Dormans (2008) argues that realism (or iconic simulation as he calls it) should not be a primary factor in game design and that it is not the function for games to be as realistic as real life (if you had to spend five years learning how to drive an accurately simulated racing car where would be the fun in that?). He suggests that there are two other forms of simulation that are useful to game designers: indexical and symbolic. Indexical simulation is described as a situation where there is a relationship between the real world and the item represented, but this may be simplified (e.g. an inventory system that uses visual object size or weight as a single limiting factor that represents all the characteristics of that object). Symbolic simulation is explained as a situation where the link between the real world and the game environment is 'arbitrary and based on convention' (Dormans, 2008: 54), for example in platform games there is a convention that walking into an enemy will kill you, while jumping on an enemy will kill it – there is no logical parallel with real life in this instance but it is understood and accepted by players of this game type.

Purpose

Another difference between educational and entertainment games is the purpose for which they have been designed, the types of gaming outcome that they embed and the link between gaming activities and intended learning objectives. Educational games, while generally aiming to be engaging and motivational, are primarily designed to facilitate learning by meeting a range of learning objectives, while entertainment games are primarily designed for enjoyment and fun. Embedding learning objectives within games so that they map on to gaming activities (i.e. playing the game achieves objectives in the game and that leads to appropriate learning) is one of the most difficult challenges for educational game designers. Many games, particularly for children, separate the game from the learning, for example by offering a mini-game as a reward for answering a set of questions correctly. However, when the actions in the game themselves are closely integrated with the learning objectives (e.g. having to go through the process of developing a photograph as part of a detective story) learning is contextualized, and more likely to be retained and transferred to other contexts. A huge challenge for designers is that of maintaining the fun and playability of the game while still achieving the learning outcomes. Ensuring an appropriate balance of fun and learning in an educational game is one of the biggest difficulties for educational game designers, but by thinking of a game as part of a larger learning package with associated activities before and after – rather than as a stand-alone activity – you can support and reinforce the learning achieved while actually playing the game.

Learning to Play the Game

The act of learning how to play an entertainment game, discovering how the interface works and the secret things that can be achieved, is often a key part of the game itself and can take a great deal of time, but adds to the fun of the game. This is generally inappropriate for educational games, where time is often limited or game-play sessions are of a fixed duration to coincide with a teaching timetable. As well as the learning gained from playing games, it is also important to acknowledge that there is the additional cognitive overhead of learning to play the game itself and, in the case of computer-based games, learning to manipulate and interact with the interface. It is important that the learning curve for being able to use the game itself is not too steep or this will detract from the benefits of the game. Many games have training levels and help functions built in to guide players through early levels and get them acclimatized to game play without having to resort to a manual (which is unlikely to be read) and it is important to consider how the game itself will be learned as part of the design. For example, in *RuneScape* players have to work through a series of training levels before playing the actual game, which show them the basics of how to interact with the game, including how to talk to people, move around, use objects and equipment and achieve tasks (see Figure 8.1).

In commercial games, learning to play is often part of the fun of playing, but it can detract from the use of the game in an educational context. Although games will often start players off on simple levels with hints and support and gradually increase in difficulty as the game progresses, this can still be time-consuming. Ways that you could consider of helping to facilitating learning include demonstrations of the interface and help functionality, development of additional support materials, and structured early tasks that allow users to familiarize themselves with the interface and the functionality as they build up confidence and expertise. Asking students to work in pairs or small groups as they start playing is a good way to foster peer learning and allow them to understand the interface together, but it is crucial to ensure that each student is able to participate in the learning experience and is not simply left as a bystander.

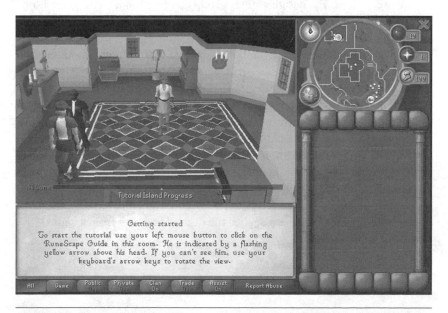

Figure 8.1 Undertaking Training in *RuneScape* (image reproduced with permission of Jagex Ltd)

Time

Another difference in the design of educational and entertainment games is the time that players are expected to spend interacting with the game. Typically in education time is extremely limited and games will either be used in restricted teaching slots or by students in their own time. Therefore, the learning within the game must be efficient (and perceived to be so by the students) and the game must be able to be played in meaningful sections that can be chunked into the time available. Commercial games can take many hours of game play to complete, but this is not a model that is generally appropriate for education.

Competition and Collaboration

Also different is the approach that games take to competition and collaboration. While competition against other people may be motivating for some learners, it is certainly not for all, and for some people a competitive game may actually be highly stressful or demotivational. Competition between individuals may lead to a focus on winning the game at all costs rather than learning from it, and therefore detract from the intended learning objectives. In line with the theories of constructivism discussed earlier in the book it is also important to look at ways in which collaboration can be built into the game design, either through interaction within the game itself or through subsequent debriefing or reflective activities. The design of inter-group competition into the game is one way to build in a competitive aspect, and so add a motivational dimension for some, while still maintaining a reason to collaborate.

Gredler (1996) describes several other factors that differentiate the design of educational games from games in general. She argues that educational games should not sanction strategies that involve questionable ethics, chance or random factors should not contribute to winning (I disagree with this point in that the use of chance factors can lead to a more interesting replayable game, but concur that chance should not outweigh skill), and that winning should depend solely on the application of subject knowledge and/or problem-solving skills (I would use predominantly rather than solely). She also makes an interesting point that problems can occur when the consequences for giving wrong answers are more interesting than those for right answers (e.g. the game of *Hangman*), which can count against the desired learning from a game.

Activity: Evaluating Entertainment Games for Learning

Select one of the three games that were introduced in the Introduction and that we have used in activities throughout this book. These three games are designed purely for entertainment.

- Consider what aspects might be detrimental to, or support, learning.
- Is the level of graphical quality sufficient?
- What support is provided for people learning the game?
- Does the game take a long time to learn how to play?
- Is it possible to break the game down into sections or chunks?
- Does it contain inappropriate content?
- Do opportunities for collaboration exist?

You will have seen that there are many differences between games that are designed explicitly for educational purposes and those that are designed for fun, and I hope I have given you a flavour of them here. In the following section, I look at the types of existing games that are available, examine different options for obtaining, modifying or developing computer games for learning, and consider their pros and cons in respect to the design issues discussed here.

Types of Existing Game for Learning

If you have decided that your preferred option is using a game that already exists for learning, rather than creating one for yourself from scratch, there are a number of different options available. In the subsections that follow I examine four options for using existing games for learning. I look first at using an entertainment game, then at the option of modifying such games. Next I examine the potential of using commercial games specifically designed for learning, and finally discuss the use of multi-user virtual worlds.

Using an Entertainment Game

A first option when obtaining a digital game for education is to use an existing commercial entertainment game, or part of such a game, for learning. Games designed for entertainment can be full-scale commercial off-the-shelf (COTS) games or smaller casual or mini-games, which are often freely available online (often online versions of casual games are provided to encourage players to pay for and download the complete version of the game). When using games designed for entertainment you are likely to have to spend more time designing activities around the game to ensure that it meets the specified learning objectives, and may be much more limited in the types of game that are actually available to meet different areas of the curriculum.

There are examples of COTS games being used effectively for learning by school-based practitioners, for example the Teaching with Games project undertaken by Futurelab and Electronic Arts (Sandford *et al.*, 2006). In the area of higher education there is a dearth of examples of using this type of game effectively for teaching, although I believe it has some potential if used creatively and pragmatically for learning in this area. As a way of showing what the potential might be for higher education, there follow brief summaries of two of the best-known examples from the school sector of using commercial off-the-shelf games.

Squire and Barab (2004) describe the use of the historical simulation game *Civilization III* as a way of supporting the teaching of history in schools. The researchers describe the learning benefits of the game in that it requires 'players to master geographic facts, anticipate the interactions among geographic processes, become fluent with historical concepts, and understand relationships among geographical, political, economic, and historical systems' (p. 1). The game was used three times a week over a six-week period in a high school classroom situation as part of an interdisciplinary world cultures course. The advantage of using a simulation game was that it allowed students to play individually to consider hypothetical historical scenarios and to develop alternative histories, better enabling them to understand the complex relationships between cause and effect. This was backed up by group discussions about the emerging situations.

Rylands (2007) used the adventure game *Myst* to support literacy among primary school children. The game was used in a classroom setting, projected on to an interactive whiteboard and discussed by the teacher and pupils as the storyline developed and game challenges were completed. Students were asked to keep reflective journals throughout detailing their thoughts and examples of good writing from the game. Supporting materials, such as maps, were also used to add to the engagement of the experience.

While these examples come from the primary and secondary school sectors, I think they both provide excellent illustrations of how COTS games can be used creatively in an educational setting, and there is potential for some of the techniques described here to be applied to higher education. The use of COTS games has the advantage of enabling students to use a high-end product which has been explicitly designed to be engaging. However, many commercial games are also expensive to purchase if a copy is required for each student and given the current business model for COTS (where publishers commission development studios to develop content and pay ongoing royalties on sales) developers insist on a minimum retail price, leaving little flexibility in respect of pricing for educational use (although older games are often available at greatly reduced rates). The growing availability of downloadable games, and casual games, available at much reduced prices, may make cost less of an issue in future.

It can also be difficult to find commercial games that exactly match the learning objectives that you want to teach, or that make appropriate bits of the game accessible without having to play through previous levels first (which may be time-consuming to complete in limited class time). The technical design of commercial games makes the separation of content from the game structure almost impossible, which makes them more difficult to use in a time-constrained classroom environment. There is often no neat cut-off point between sections of game play, and use of the game may have to be designed into several sessions. In many cases realism in commercial games is sacrificed for the sake of playability (e.g. in forensic science investigation games, processes may be modified or truncated) but as long as this is recognized it can still work as a learning experience leading to discussion and debate. Another difficulty is that the teacher needs to be familiar with the game and to have ensured that the content is appropriate throughout; given the length of many commercial games this can be extremely time-consuming. Commercial gaming environments may also have complex interfaces, extensive functionality and a long learning period, which may detract from the intended learning objectives. The long time taken to complete many games may also be far greater than a typical teaching timetable.

Even given these limitations of commercial entertainment games, I believe there is still potential in the higher education context, although at present very few examples exist. In Table 8.1 I have used four of the games presented in this book as examples, giving an indication of how they could be used for learning. These are, however, only ideas intended to stimulate your own thinking on the use of commercial games.

As well as the option of using full-scale commercial games, there are also many smaller mini-games available, usually for free, from the web. These have the advantage of being quicker to play, requiring less computing resources to run and being easier to integrate into a teaching schedule. However these types of games also have lower production values and may not be as robust and well-tested as large-scale games. There is also an issue when using any free software that it may not be available when you require it (e.g. the website is unavailable) so, in this scenario, it is a good idea to communicate with the owners of the host site (particularly if the game is critical to a particular area of teaching), who will usually be delighted that you want to use their game and happy to let you know if there is likely to be any downtime.

Table 8.1 Potential Uses of Commercial Entertainment Computer Games in Higher Education

Game	Description	Learning areas
Age of Empires	A real-time strategy game where players have to support their tribes to develop through several stages of civilization by developing technologies, conquering enemies and exploration.	Strategy. History. Politics.
CSI: Crime Scene Investigation	Crime scene procedural game in which players have to find, collect and analyse evidence in order to solve mysteries.	Forensic analysis. Scientific techniques. Analysis and evaluation.
In Memoriam	Adventure game mystery that utilizes the Internet as well as the game environment to enable players to solve puzzles and progress the story.	Web navigation. New media literacy. Information search and evaluation.
And Then There Were None	Adventure game in which the main character has to solve a crime by collecting statements and evidence through solving a series of puzzles.	Problem-solving. Lateral thinking.

Modifying Existing Entertainment Games

The growing trend towards modifying existing games software for use in education (de Freitas, 2007) may provide one way to address some of the issues around customization of commercial games and help to ensure links between learning objectives and gaming activities. Some gaming environments now come with creation software that allows teachers, or students, to develop their own add-ons such as new storylines or game areas). This reduces the time required to develop educational games and the expertise required – although it is still not a trivial process. Modification of games may still be expensive, as it often requires the ownership of the original game and may still require a range of technical skills, but will enable the production of a professional-looking product.

An excellent example of the use of a modding engine for learning, again in the schools sector, involved the use of modifications to the *Neverwinter Nights* role-playing game. In this instance primary school pupils were given support to develop their own additions to the game as a way of teaching narrative and storytelling skills (Robertson & Howells, 2008).

Using Existing Educational Games

If you are considering using existing games, then as well as the option of selecting a game designed for entertainment, there is also the option of choosing one designed specifically for education. There are a number of commercial gaming environments explicitly designed for learning. However, these can be also expensive to purchase and are often still difficult to customize to particular teaching situations and curricula.

One academic field that has a longer history than most in the use of games is the area of business, management and marketing. There is a clear link between their practical and applied nature, based on numerical models, and the potential for computer games-based learning to allow students to practise in a range of different scenarios. The *Marketplace* business game was used by Whitton and Hynes (2006) at Napier University. In teams, students were asked to take up the role of companies producing, selling and marketing computer systems, and had to make a number of decisions at the end of each decision period. The teams were involved with a range of marketing activities around selling computer systems – applying theory previously studied. Greco and Murgia (2007) used *Win Win Manager*, an online multi-user business game that focused on developing negotiation skills in particular. This game allows pairs of players to negotiate anonymously online in one of ten different scenarios and to receive a score (and feedback) at the end of each negotiation session depending on how well they had performed.

In some areas, other educationalists have produced bespoke games for learning in particular curriculum areas, which they may be willing to let you use or adapt, either free or for a small fee. When researching potential games in your own discipline, it is worth doing some research in your own field to see if any appropriate games exist within the academic sphere.

Using Virtual Worlds

A fourth, and growingly popular, option is the use of existing virtual worlds and multi-user virtual environments (MUVEs) such as *Second Life*, or harnessing the potential for learning in massively multiplayer online role-playing games (MMORPGs). However, to date, the majority of research on the learning potential of MMORPGs has looked at incidental learning that occurs from playing rather than using the game in a structured teaching environment. Although there are as yet no examples of MMORPGs being used as part of a higher education curriculum, studies of leisure users of have found evidence of collaborative learning and development of communities of practice (Steinkuehler, 2004), as well as the potential for learning a range of group skills, including the etiquette of meeting people, group management, cooperation and social interaction (Ducheneaut & Moore, 2005).

There are more examples of the use of *Second Life* to support learning in higher education. Livingstone (2007) describes the use of a multi-user virtual environment (MUVE) combining *Second Life* with a traditional virtual learning environment (VLE) to support student learning. The environment provides tools to support reflection, emotional content in communication, assessment and planning. Childress and Braswell (2006) describe the use of the environment to support cooperative learning at university.

There is some debate about whether an environment such as *Second Life* can actually be classified as a game in itself, but I chose to include it here for completeness because of the immersive nature of the environment and the game-like graphics and interaction it employs. These massive online worlds allow the interaction of hundreds of thousands of players in real-time in virtual spaces; players can manipulate objects, solve quests, create and join groups, or work with others. Some virtual worlds also allow users to create their own spaces and objects, which provides potential for creativity and the development of personalized spaces. Hollins and Robbins (2008) have identified what they term as the 'educational affordances' of MUVEs, namely: the fact that identity is fluid and that students can safely experiment with their identities as they learn, the ability to create and explore virtual space, the scope for a variety of user-centred activities to take place, the scripting tools that offer potential for learning programming, and meeting and collaborating with others as part of a community.

The advantages of using these types of virtual world for learning are that they already exist, have a low development overhead, and are often cheap or free to use at a basic level. However, there are still problems associated with using these worlds, which include the lack of privacy from other users who can wander into teaching spaces, the bad reputation that has built up over certain types of behaviour in these environments (e.g. violence in MMORPGs and the overtly commercial nature and sexual behaviour in MUVEs), and the high-specification machines and internet connections required to effectively run these applications. A key advantage of these environments is their intrinsic collaborative nature, enabling users to communicate with one another and work together to achieve collaborative tasks.

Obtaining Existing Games

Once you have a rough idea of the type of game you want to use, how you plan to use it to teach and an initial specification for what you require (e.g. by completing the activities detailed in Chapter 6), the next step is carry out a structured search for any games available. It is important to have an idea of your concept specification before you start to look for a game because it is very easy to get sidetracked by games with high production values and playability that do not necessarily meet your required learning objectives. Having a specification of requirements to check back against will help to avoid this.

It is also entirely possible that you will not be able to find an appropriate game to meet your needs or that any game you do find will not be feasible in your context owing, for example, to prohibitive costs or high hardware requirements. In this case you could consider either re-examining your requirements or investigating the possibility of having the game created from scratch.

I often find that the best way to start looking for a particular game is to start with a simple Google search. There are so many websites available in different domains and subject areas that it would be impossible to list them all here. What I have attempted to do in the following subsections is simply to provide a selection of websites that I find useful for finding games (and for giving me ideas if I am creating a games from scratch). Rather than list hundreds of sites, I have aimed to give one or two examples of the types of sites you could look for – I am certain that if you undertake your own search you will find many, many more. I have provided brief summaries and web addresses here, and updates will be available from the accompanying website. If you do come across a site or resource that you find particularly useful, please let me know and I will add it to the links online.

Game Review Sites

There are many online sites that cater for reviewing all types of commercial games. The one that I have highlighted here focuses on adventure games only, one genre that I think is particularly appropriate for learning in higher education. It provides reviews of a range of different adventure games.

www.justadventure.com

Casual Game Sites

Casual gaming sites offer a wide range of games. While many may not be appropriate for learning at the level of higher education, they can provide lots of examples and give you lots of ideas. Two of the most popular casual gaming sites, which both offer free online games and download games (at a small cost) are:

www.shockwave.com
www.bigfishgames.com

Free Game Sites

Like the games on casual gaming sites, many of the games on free sites will be inappropriate for learning, however I think they are still a good source of inspiration and ideas. You can find free mini-games and casual games at the following sites:

www.miniclip.com
www.electrotank.com

The E4 games site is also an excellent resource for accessing hundreds of free internet games in a variety of genres.

www.e4.com/games

Educational Game Sites

There are many educational game sites that offer games for children, but there is much less available for adult learning. Caspian Learning is a UK-based company that specializes in the development of immersive simulations.

www.caspianlearning.co.uk

Marketplace and Win Win Manager offer two of the business simulations described in this chapter.

www.marketplace-simulation.com
www.wwmanager.it/uk/

Virtual Worlds

Probably the most famous virtual world, particularly in the sphere of education, is *Second Life*. You can sign up and find out more on their website.

www.secondlife.com

Another virtual world that has been used actively in education for some time is *Active Worlds*.

www.activeworlds.com

Of course there are a great many other online resources for finding educational games and their number is growing all the time. However, I hope that these sites will give you a taster of the types of resources out there.

Don't be too surprised if you can't find the perfect game for your situation in half an hour. While there are a lot of options available, you will still need to do a lot of searching and evaluating before you find a game that meets your needs (and it's entirely possible that one doesn't exist). In the next chapter I will look at ways in which you can design and develop your own games from scratch.

Activity: Finding a Game to Meet Your Game Concept Specification

In Chapter 6 there was an activity to create a game concept specification. If you haven't completed it already I suggest you do so before undertaking this activity. With your concept specification in mind:

• Spend 20–30 minutes looking at some of the websites described above.
• Try carrying out a search on Google (or your preferred search engine).

Can you find any games that meet, or partially meet, your concept specification?

Chapter Summary

This chapter started by looking at the differences that you should be aware of between games designed for education and those designed specifically for learning.

It then looked at the advantages and disadvantages of four options for using existing games: entertainment games (both commercial off-the-shelf and casual games), modification of entertainment games, commercial games for learning, and the use of multi-user virtual worlds.

The chapter concluded by presenting a range of web resources for obtaining games.

Further Reading

S. de Freitas, C. Savill-Smith & J. Attewell (2006). *Computer Games and Simulations for Adult Learning: Case Studies from Practice*. London: Learning and Skills Network (retrieved Jan. 2009 from http://www.lsneducation.org.uk/pubs/Pages/062546.aspx). This provides a number of good examples of the use of commercial games for learning, albeit limited in respect to higher order skills.

http://www.eduserv.org.uk/foundation/studies/slsnapshots – The Eduserv Foundation has produced a series of reports on current use of *Second Life* in the UK FE and HE sectors.

CHAPTER 9

Developing New Digital Games
for Learning

In this chapter I explore the potential for developing new games for learning in higher education, first looking at the benefits and drawbacks of creating games from scratch and considering the range of skills required in order to create your own games. I then go on to look at how to develop a functional specification for your game and talk about techniques for creating a balanced game for learning. Finally, I introduce a number of tools and technologies that you can use to create your own games.

In order to create a game for yourself (or work with others to create one on your behalf) I recommend further developing the initial concept specification (created in the final activity of Chapter 6) to produce a more detailed functional specification that will define more exactly what your game is and enable you to share your vision with others. This allows you to describe exactly what you want the game to do and how you want users to interact with it. In the later part of this chapter I look at the sort of information you might want to include in this functional specification (again drawing on the *Time Capsule* example used previously). I also introduce some more of my own research to offer some advice on how to structure games for learning and how to create engagement in games.

Creating New Games for Learning

Rather than using or modifying pre-existing games in your learning and teaching situation, a second option is to develop (or have developed for you) your own games for teaching, such as the action-adventure game developed to teach basic literacy skills to adults (Kambouri *et al.*, 2006). While this may seem like a much more difficult option, it has the advantage that you can have a game designed to meet exactly the learning objectives you require, ensuring that it meets the practical needs of the teaching session and is designed to match the curriculum.

However, despite the clear benefits in terms of having a game specifically designed, there are a number of disadvantages associated with producing your own game. Although a range of development applications and toolkits exist, which make the development processes easier, a whole range of specialist skills are needed in terms of programming, interface design, game design and graphical input; and the whole development process is still likely to be relatively expensive and time-consuming. Even though there is the opportunity to create bespoke games to match your needs, there may still be pressure to make them usable in as many contexts as possible (particularly if the game development is externally funded or you are working with others) so you may still have to make compromises. They may end up being not quite right for any particular context, and may still be difficult to customize.

Given that commercial games producers spend millions on development, it is virtually impossible for a game you develop yourself to reach that kind of production value, and some experts in the game-based learning field would argue that graphics and game-play quality equivalent to that of entertainment games is essential for players to be engaged. As I said previously, in general I disagree on this point – particularly in the context of higher education – and believe that it is not the graphical quality that is of primary importance (although it must be adequate) but it is the game design and the quality of the interaction that is crucial for engendering engagement (although there may be some exceptions, particularly with student groups with large numbers of hard core gamers who are used to, and expect, high-end graphics). A game produced on a lower budget will necessarily have much lower production values in terms of graphics and visual appeal than a commercial product; and this may also have an impact on the expectations of learners and their motivations to participate. Jenkins (2002) argues that most educational software is of poor quality, badly edited and unprofessional, and I would agree that this is often – but not always – the case. It is unlikely, however, that the amounts of money spent on commercial software will ever be viable in education, and I feel that rather than focusing on developing something that can never compete with a commercial game, it is important that resources are focused on ensuring that educational games, particularly for adults, are well designed in terms of playability and learning. While this means perhaps that there is less of a hurdle when it comes to the graphics, good game design is not easy and should not be overlooked as a crucial aspect.

There are really three options for creating bespoke games: by yourself as an individual, by an in-house team, or by an external team or company. Creating games yourself has the advantage of allowing you a great deal of control but unless you have an extremely wide skill-set it may be difficult to produce something of acceptable quality (in terms of graphical feel, design, system robustness and game play). Using a small team of developers and designers will overcome these problems – but again you are lucky if you have that type of resource available. A third option is to have a game developed by an external professional team, which starts to become extremely expensive and would almost certainly require external funding. For those reasons I won't dwell on this final option here but will focus on the other two.

A growing number of game development engines, produced by the industry in order to address the spiralling costs of game development, are also available to educators at increasingly affordable costs. In parallel to this, a number of open-source tools and technologies can be used, though they require a degree of technical competency. This can keep development costs down but the skills of game production professionals, such as graphic artists and animators, are still expensive and required for a truly professional product.

One solution to the problem of developing a gaming environment that is fit-for-purpose, customizable and relatively inexpensive in terms of development time and manpower cost is the alternate reality game (ARG). This type of game has the advantage that it can be developed using a whole range of freely available online tools and websites and does not need to have a high level of technical expertise to be able to be easily developed.

Another option in terms of the development of computer games in education is, instead of viewing students as players of games (or merely consumers of content), to take the view that they can learn by developing or creating games themselves. Rieber *et al.* (1998) argue that learning by building games can be at least as effective a way to learn as traditional methods, if not more effective, while Gee (2003) puts forward the case that active, critical learning should lead to learners becoming designers, either by physically designing extensions to the game or by cognitively extending the game design and using that to inform their play. The easy availability of game development tools and modification engines makes this a more feasible option, but still some level of technical and design expertise is required by students. While I highlight this as an option, I will not go into this concept in any great detail.

Although there are a number of options for producing digital games for learning, as presented in this section, it is unlikely in the context of higher education, with limited budgets and development expertise available, that it will ever be possible to obtain a game that is absolutely perfect for any given teaching situation. Essentially I feel that the use of digital games for learning will have to be undertaken with a high degree of pragmatism, and this again highlights the importance of not seeing a game as a stand-alone activity but as part of a learning package of activities.

To give you a flavour of the types of game that can be created by practitioners in higher education, I would like to give you a couple of examples at this point. Ebner and Holzinger (2007) provide an excellent example of a bespoke game used within lectures; they developed an online simulation game to support the teaching of civil engineering concepts through their application. The *Internal Force Master* provides problems based around the theory of structures, and students are required to solve the problems in a short time, which allows them to test their understandings of the concepts involved (see Figure 9.1).

A second example is provided by Pimenidis (2007), who developed a computer game for library induction. The game presents a range of realistic tasks and aims to provide an engaging alternative method of orienting students to the university library and the range of services that are on offer (see Figure 9.2).

There are lots of options in terms of the available technologies you may decide to use to create your game, but at the same time a number of skills need to be available for design and development. In the following section, I

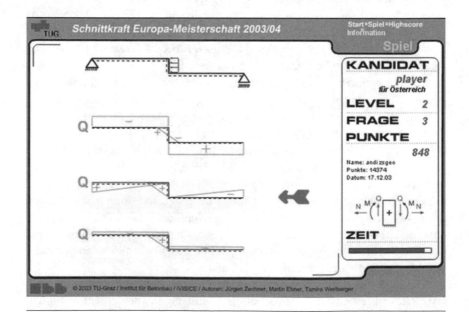

Figure 9.1 The *Internal Force Master* (image reproduced with permission of Andreas Holzinger)

Figure 9.2 The *Library Induction Game* (image reproduced with permission of Elias Pimenidis)

will examine the types of skills required for educational game development to provide an overview of what you need if you decide to go down this route.

Skills Required for Game Creation

In order to create an educational game from scratch, there are a range of skills that are required. A single individual would be very talented to possess all of them (although it is not unusual that a person has more than one) so it is likely that you will want to work with other people. The following list considers the range of skills and expertise required to be able to create different types of computer game from scratch.

- *Subject expert*. This is the person who knows about the subject matter that is required to be covered in the game and has experience of actually teaching it to students; who knows what the learning objectives are and what areas the students are likely to find difficult.
- *Educationalist*. This is a person with understanding of learning in general, and online and game-based learning in particular, with an appreciation of the differences between commercial and educational games, the age group and backgrounds of the learners to be catered

for, and how to design effective digital games for education.
    The educationalist and subject expert will also have an insight into
the other types of activities that can be used to support the game-based
learning package.

- *Game designer*. This is someone with an understanding of the elements
  required to make games fun and engaging, to keep players interested and
  encourage them to keep playing. The game designer need not specialize
  in educational game design but can offer the perspectives of designing
  compelling narrative, game play and plot.
- *Programmer*. This will be an individual who can use the development
  software to create the game as specified by the other team members.
- *Interaction designer*. This is a person with a knowledge of interaction
  design and user-centred design who can help to ensure that the game is
  designed to be as usable as possible (usability and user-centred design are
  discussed in the final chapter in this part of the book).
- *Graphic designer*. While I have said previously that I don't feel that graphics
  are as critical an aspect as the overall game design, I still think that a certain
  acceptable level of graphic design is essential for the game to be seen as
  professional. For this reason I think that a person with graphic design skill
  is an important member of the team.
- *Writer*. Depending on the type of game you plan to produce, and the
  balance between game-play and storytelling within that game, you may
  find a dedicated writer to be a useful addition to the team.

The types of role presented here come from my experience in bespoke
game and interactive multimedia development. Of course they will differ from
the roles in a commercial gaming organization, mainly due to the far smaller
budgets available, and in practice not every role will be essential for every
project. However, this list is intended to provide an indication of the types of
expertise required before you start a game-based learning project.

Developing a Functional Specification

In order to take your game idea forward from the initial concept specification
developed in Chapter 6, I would recommend that you develop a more
complete functional specification. This will enable you to evaluate the types of
development environments available and identify which of the skills discussed
in the previous section you need in order to be able to create the game you
want.

    A functional specification describes in more detail exactly what you want
the game to do, how you want players to interact with the objects in the game
and with each other, and what you want the game to look like. In the functional

specification you should consider all the game elements that you want to include in your game and how they will work (not all elements will be present in all games). The key areas that you should consider are: the environment, navigation, tasks that players have to achieve, characters, objects, object interaction, player interaction and status information.

- *Environment.* A description of the game world and the locations that exist within the world. You can use this to give an idea of how you would like the game to look. For a game that does not use a virtual location (such as the *Time Capsule*) you should describe the playing environment.
- *Navigation.* If the play requires movement through different locations in the game (or screens), you need to consider how you want players to navigate through the different game areas, and what additional navigation tools (such as a map or compass) might be required.
- *Tasks.* This is what you want the players to be able to do to complete the game. If you have previously undertaken a mapping of learning objectives and game actions (the first activity in Chapter 6), this will provide you with a starting point.
- *Characters.* Identify whether players will take on the role of characters, whether they will have a choice of role and how their characters will be represented in the game (e.g. will avatars be used?). You should also consider whether there will be non-player characters in the game that players have to interact with, and detail who they are and what their function is.
- *Objects.* Document what objects will be available at what points in the game and what their purpose will be. For example, in an adventure game a bucket may be used to contain water. How much detail you want to go into at this stage will depend on how closely the specific objects are linked to the tasks to be achieved (in the example below, I just knew at this stage that a certain number of objects were required but not exactly what they were).
- *Object interaction.* This is how the players will interact with objects and the actions that they can carry out on them (e.g. pick them up, put them down, make them interact with the environment, place them in an inventory) and how objects can interact with other objects.
- *Player interaction.* This includes all the ways that players can interact with each other, for example the ways in which they can communicate and actions that one player can take that will affect another player (e.g. in the *Time Capsule*, if one player selects an object other players will see this selection).
- *Status information.* Ways of providing players with information about the current state of the game and with feedback about their progress, e.g. timers, scores, progress bars and feedback messages.

Your functional specification may be a relatively short document or may extend for many pages depending on how large and complex you want the eventual game to be. Table 9.1 shows a basic functional specification for the *Time Capsule*.

Table 9.1 Functional Specification for *The Time Capsule* Game

	Functionality required
Environment	Players need to be able to see the potential array of objects for possible selection for the time capsule. They need to be able to bring up detailed information about each object, including a picture and the price. Players need to be aware of the other people playing and have a mechanism for communicating with them and reviewing previous conversations.
Navigation	Play takes place on a single screen so players do not need to navigate between game locations.
Tasks	Each player has a different background and needs that they have to familiarize themselves with and be able to communicate to the other players. Players have to agree as a group on six items from thirty to be placed in a time capsule. The group must also ensure that their selected items do not go over the allocated budget. They must make a decision within a set time period.
Characters	Each player will be automatically allocated one of four roles. Information is provided about each character's needs and desires, which will be viewable only by that character.
Objects	Thirty different objects will be available to be selected. Each will have a different value and a different attractiveness to each player (this will be detailed in individual player information).
Object interaction	Players can select and de-select objects. Players can see all the objects that are currently selected.
Player interaction	See the characters that are taking part. Communicate with other players in real time with text. See when an item has been selected by another player. Have a mechanism for reaching a final agreement with other players.
Status information	See the time remaining. See the number of items currently selected. See the total cost of items so far. See when a player wants to bring about agreement. See when agreement has/has not been reached.

The example provided is necessarily short for the sake of illustration, but it is up to you how much detail you wish to go into at this stage. Remember that your functional specification will be the main way of communicating your ideas to others. You should be prepared to make several iterations of your functional specification and amend and adapt it as necessary as you go through various stages of development, so don't worry about getting everything complete or perfect at this stage. You should view this as a work in progress that will allow you to keep track of your ideas and think through aspects of the game mechanics.

Activity: Creating a Functional Specification for Your Own Game

If you haven't already completed the learning objective mapping and developed a concept specification in Chapter 6, I suggest that you complete those activities now.

Use the headings provided above and your concept specification to create an initial functional specification for your own game.

At this stage you may find that you are not able to complete the entire specification. There may be areas that are still not clear to you or that you need to think about in the future. The very act of undertaking a first iteration of the specification will help you to identify areas that need further thought. You may find it very useful at this point to talk through your ideas with someone else. In the next section I will introduce some ideas of game balance and playability that may lead you to refine your functional specification further.

Creating a Balanced Game for Learning

As well as thinking about the functionality you want your game to have at this stage, it is also a good idea to think about how you are going to ensure playability. In terms of educational games in the context of higher education, there are two areas from my own research that I think are useful to look at when thinking about how the game can be balanced to ensure that it is playable for a whole range of different students with different backgrounds, experience with games and motivations for playing.

My research on motivation highlighted the importance of students being able to start to play the game quickly and to be able to make swift and steady improvements quickly so that they have the perception of being good at the game. Another issue highlighted was that of getting stuck within the game. While from an educational point of view an activity that students find challenging and have to work at is valuable, in games players can reach a problem that they find insoluble and will simply give up if they feel that the game system is not treating them fairly.

It is important that players can start to play the game quickly without having to spend too long learning the rules, etiquette and parameters (particularly in an educational setting where time may be limited). An activity that is difficult to get into, without proper helpful instructions, detracts very much from engagement; quick initial gratification from games is important to draw players in and to keep them playing. There are a number of techniques that computer games can use to allow players to start playing quickly, achieve initial goals rapidly and facilitate the transformation from novice to expert. Houser and DeLoach (1998) suggest seven features of games that can ease this transition:

- The use of an attract mode or demonstration with graphics or video that display when the game is not being played to get the attention of potential users and demonstrate what can be accomplished within the game and how it is played.
- Clearly stated goals that are explicit and easily understandable by the players.
- Concise instructions, provided at intervals throughout the game when required by the user (rather than all provided up front when they are out of context).
- Transparency of controls and functionality of the interface, with only the controls that are currently available and appropriate to access at a given time being able to be accessed at that point.
- Performance coaching throughout the game, with necessary information and motivational aids provided when required.
- The use of training wheels that let users be successful from the beginning of the game and allow them to gain greater control of the interface and functionality as they gain experience and confidence.
- The provision of consistent feedback through audio and visual cues and continuous scoring.

For example, in *RuneScape*, players can increase in skill levels very quickly during the training period while in *NotPron* the first three levels are relatively trivial, to give players an idea about what the game involves, but the puzzles quickly escalate in difficulty (see Figure 9.3).

The issue of getting stuck for a long time at a certain point, for instance reaching a plateau in skill level or being unable to solve a puzzle, and not being able to progress, was seen as demotivating, particularly for this group of adult learners who place an extremely high value on their time and do not want to waste it going around in circles. There is a difference between difficulty and appropriate challenge, where something is hard but achievable, and getting stuck, reaching an impasse and becoming frustrated. Getting the correct level of challenge for all players is, I think, one of the most difficult aspects of

Figure 9.3 The Easy Early Levels of *NotPron* Provide Quick Rewards (image reproduced with permission of David Münnich)

designing effective digital games for learning. Ways of supporting game play can involve offering different levels of challenge, and making this explicit to players, offering hints and clues at different levels, providing information based on time elapsed (so if a challenge hasn't been completed in a set time it can be made easier), and developing collaborative communities around the game so that players are encouraged to work together and help one another out of difficulties. For example, *NotPron* provides a variety of ways to get help when players get stuck, including explicit hints, hidden hints and support forums.

The other thing to consider when designing a game for learning is why people get engaged in games and why they play them. From my experience, and particularly from my recent work in alternate reality games, there are six factors that lead to engagement with games, with different factors being more crucial for different people. These are shown in Figure 9.4.

- *Completion.* Some players will simply want to complete the game and achieve all the tasks or challenges, similar to wanting to complete a jigsaw to see the full picture. This can be facilitated using techniques like making all the tasks apparent up front and allowing them to be checked off, or linking subtasks to some overall reward such as completing a picture.

Figure 9.4 Factors That Facilitate Engagement with Educational Games

- *Competition.* An element of competition can motivate some people, although it may turn off others, so it has to be applied carefully and should not be too overt, or linked to the overall rewards of completing the game. Adding a leader board or high scores list will enable players to see how they are performing in relation to others.
- *Narrative.* A compelling ongoing story with an element of mystery can help to stimulate curiosity and keep students engaged, as well as embedding activities within a purposeful context. Fantasy narrative may be less appropriate in this context but it will really depend upon the particular student group.
- *Puzzle-solving.* Ongoing puzzles, riddles and problems that need to be solved also serve to stimulate curiosity and heighten engagement. These should start relatively easy so that players are drawn into the game and receive early gratification from playing, but can then get gradually more difficult as students become more experienced.
- *Community.* Supporting play outwith the game and encouraging players to talk to one another and work collaboratively will be motivational for some players. Ways of facilitating this include the provision of forums or other online community space, and tasks that require collaboration (either explicitly or because they are too difficult for one person to achieve alone).
- *Creativity.* The opportunity for players to be creative, either through lateral thinking and creative problem-solving or through the creation of their own artefacts within the game (e.g. creating posters, video, or stories) allows people to become more immersed in the game and shape its direction.

In terms of creating a balanced game, thinking about these six elements can allow you to ensure that you are catering for as wide a range of student motivations and preferences as possible. For the *ViolaQuest* alternate reality game we tried to ensure that each of these elements was catered for: while the narrative, puzzle-solving and community are intrinsic to the game design, we used a grid to present challenges that when completed provided an additional picture clue to support the completion motivation (see Figure 9.5), added a leader board to support competition and developed a photographic challenge to support student creativity.

Narrative is one element that may be particularly difficult to get right, particularly in terms of getting the right balance between game play and story. Dansky (2007) highlights three functions of narrative in games: to increase the player's immersion with the game and stimulate curiosity, to reward the player with answers and surprising and unsuspected events, and to enable the player

Figure 9.5 Supporting the Completion Motivation in *ViolaQuest*

to identify and emotionally connect with the characters. The context in which you situate your game needs to be carefully thought out in order to ensure that the narrative does not detract from the learning objectives or put some people off playing because they consider the game to be inappropriate (e.g. games with a fantasy setting can be off-putting for many people). This is particularly important for the acceptability of using games with adults. I like to view the story in an educational game as the glue that holds the activities together and draws the player in, rather than the central element of the game.

Activity: Ensuring Your Game is Balanced

If you haven't undertaken the previous activity and created a draft functional specification for a game of your own, I suggest you complete that activity now.

Go back to the functional specification and consider:

*   How can players get started quickly and make fast initial progress?
*   What can players do when they get stuck?
*   Have you included ways to support people with an instinct for completion, competition, narrative, puzzle-solving, community and creativity?
*   Are there elements you could add to improve the overall balance of the game?

Make any required changes to your functional specification.

Not all elements will be appropriate for all types of games (for instance you may decide that you do not want your game to be competitive in any way), and the final functionality is a decision you must make for yourself. Considering the right blend of elements at this stage will help you identify any points that you may not have previously considered and allow you to incorporate additional functionality requirements early on in the game design process. It is worth noting, however, that not all games need to include all elements; some may focus on the story or characters while others may have a larger element of puzzle-solving or competition, but knowing what elements can contribute to the balance of a game will help you make informed decisions about how you choose to design your own.

Software for Creating Games

There are a variety of different types of software available for creating digital games. In this section I will briefly discuss the different options; but, in order to ensure that this book isn't already out of date by the time it is published, I will avoid going into detail about version numbers, specific functionalities offered or actual links to sites where software can be bought or downloaded. However, all of this information will be made available, and kept up to date on the supporting website. What this book also does not cover is how to actually develop games using a specific development environment or programming language – there are plenty of books and web resources that do that already – but it does aim to give you an overview of the options available so that you can have an idea where to start.

There are several different alternative systems for game creation: multimedia development environments and programming languages; game development environments; e-learning software development tools; and modding environments. Examples of these are all discussed in the following subsections. Other considerations include whether you want your game to be available online or whether you want your users to have to install it, whether it is stand-alone or networked (single-user or multi-player) and what types of computer and operating systems you expect your students to be using.

Programming Languages

If you have the programming expertise, it is possible to create games in languages such as Java (www.java.com). Java is a programming language that enables the creation of web-based games (as well as stand-alone games). The advantage of programming directly in a language is that you have more control over the code; the disadvantage is the high level of programming expertise required and the difficulty of developing graphical interfaces.

Multimedia Development Environments

Multimedia development environments are not specifically designed for games, but are often ideal environments in which to create them, and this is one of their common uses. They provide a variety of visual tools and elements, usually supported by a robust programming language. Again, some skill is needed in programming to create complex applications, but the variety of wizards and code libraries now available with these environments means that they are much more accessible to novices and non-programmers.

A word of caution: the ease of use of these environments has meant that it is now possible for most people to create interactive applications easily. While it is deceptively easy to create something in practice, do not be fooled into thinking that the design (both of the interface and the game play) is equally easy.

Adobe Flash (www.adobe.com/products/flash) is one of the leading interactive content creation tools on the market. It is relatively expensive to buy but there are educational versions available. Flash provides a combination of drawing palate, animation features, and creation of interactive elements, all supported by a robust programming language.

Game-Development Environments

A third option is using development environments that are specifically designed to create digital games. These have the advantage that they are relatively easy to design in, while having a range of functionality built in to enhance game play. Again, they may require some levels of expertise for developers.

Adventure Game Studio (www.adventuregamestudio.co.uk) is a free software application that allows you to create your own point-and-click adventure game. Point-and-click games are essentially a very simple form of adventure that involves solving puzzles like getting out of locked rooms; they may make use of an inventory and simple dialogue.

Dark Basic (darkbasic.thegamecreators.com) is a relatively inexpensive 3D games programming language, which has been specifically designed for the creation of a variety of types of game both by professionals and keen amateurs.

Inform (www.inform-fiction.org) is a text-based design system for interactive fiction, with which the user can create adventure games similar to those popular in the 1980s. The advantage of a text-based system is that it allows the focus of the game to be on game play rather than graphics, but may be discriminatory to some students (e.g. those with dyslexia or a preference for visual learning).

E-Learning Software

Online learning software provides a number of options for developing games, but may involve creative use and workarounds as it is not expressly designed for this purpose. The types of games created in this way, I would argue, will tend to be more basic, superficial and supporting of the lower level learning outcomes of retention and repetition, unless cleverly designed. Tools exist such as Quandary (www.halfbakedsoftware.com/quandary.php) for producing action mazes, or Raptivity (www.raptivity.com) that allows the user to create basic gaming interactions.

Modding Environments

As mentioned in the previous chapter, there are a range of games that have engines built in that allow them to make modifications and extensions to the original game. These require less technical expertise but do require that the player (and developer) owns and is familiar with the original game that has been modified.

The most common genre for supporting modifications is first-person shooters, which I would argue is possibly one of the least appropriate genres for learning in higher education. However, there are role-playing games that now offer modification engines, such as *Neverwinter Nights* (nwn.bioware.com).

I have aimed here to provide you with a short overview of the different types of software available. A comprehensive list of development software for games can be found at:

www.ambrosine.com/resource.html

Although I have aimed not to go into any technical detail about specific environments, in the next chapter I will describe what I think is the ideal development process for creating appropriate games for learning – user-centred iterative design. I examine some of the things you need to consider in order to make your game usable and accessible regardless of the technology you have chosen to develop it in.

Chapter Summary

In this chapter I looked at the arguments for creating your own games for learning, and the advantages and disadvantages (as compared to using an existing game). I then considered the type of skills that you will need to develop a game for yourself, including subject expert, educationalist, game designer, programmer, interaction designer and graphic designer.

I looked at how you can create a more detailed functional specification considering game design elements such as the environment, navigation, tasks, characters, objects, object interaction, player interaction and status information. Aspects of creating a balanced game and elements of game design were considered, in particular: completion, competition, narrative, puzzle-solving, community and creativity.

Finally a number of pieces of development software were presented, including programming languages, multimedia development environments, game development environments, e-learning software and modding environments.

Further Reading

C. Bateman (Ed.) (2007). *Game Writing: Narrative Skills for Videogames*. Boston, MA: Charles River Media. Recommended if you are interested in ways to develop narrative within digital games.

M. Krawczyk & J. Novak (2006). *Game Development Essentials: Game Story and Character Development*. Clifton Park, NY: Delmar Learning. Also recommended – of particular interest are Chapter 3 on 'Building your story' and Chapter 7 on 'Verbal character development'.

S. Salen & E. Zimmerman (2004). *Rules of Play: Game Design Fundamentals*. Cambridge, MA: MIT Press. Chapter 24, 'The play of pleasure', examines how games can be designed to bring pleasure. This is well worth reading to gain insights into the perspective of design for entertainment as well as gaining a deeper understanding of engagement.

CHAPTER **10**

Evaluating Digital Games for Learning

In this chapter I introduce the idea of iterative user-centred design with ongoing evaluation as a method for ensuring that games for learning are appropriate. I also examine a variety of ways in which you can evaluate digital games to ensure that they are fit-for-purpose, usable by the student population and accessible.

I first discuss the importance of taking a user-centred design approach to the development of games for learning, describe a number of methods for gaining feedback from users and look at the process of developing an evaluation plan.

This chapter also looks at the different types of evaluation that exist, focusing primarily on diagnostic evaluations that you can carry out on any game that you are considering using for learning. In the second half of the chapter I present a set of guidelines that you can use to evaluate the usability of games for learning and highlight issues that may need to be addressed.

Iterative User-Centred Design

If you want any game you are developing to be as appropriate and useful for your students as possible then it is important to involve them in evaluation throughout the design and development process. The process of iterative user-centred design supports this user involvement at different stages and allows you to get ongoing feedback so that you can identify problems early and make adjustments to the game design and interface as required.

It is my belief that user-centred design is of critical importance in the design of computer systems in general and of games in particular, especially in the design of games for learning, when the way in which the players interact with the game can seriously influence the type and level of learning that takes place. There are many books covering user-centred design in great detail so I'm not going to try to provide a comprehensive analysis here, but simply give you an idea of the importance of ongoing evaluation and testing, different aspects that can be evaluated and some methods for carrying out evaluations during the game development process.

User-centred design, at its most basic, simply involves putting end-users at the heart of the software design process and looking at the ways in which they use and interact with the software and systems that are being developed. I think that a development methodology that utilizes a user-centred design process, which is implemented by undertaking iterative usability testing throughout the process, is essential because it allows issues to be identified quickly and rectified, it involves users in the process throughout and can spark creative ideas that the developers or designers never considered and, ultimately, it leads to a better designed game.

Some areas of the design process we have already looked at in earlier chapters, such as understanding your students and the context of use. In this section I will focus on the types of evaluation that can take place during the building phase of development, once the initial design and functional specification is complete (although there are likely to be, in practice, further changes to the game design as feedback from users is received).

As mentioned throughout this book, the acceptability of any game to its target users is very important. If possible, it is always a good idea to gauge the appropriateness of game-based learning with the particular student group with which you intend to use it. If it is a student group you know well or are familiar with, this can be as straightforward as talking to a sample of students and finding out their opinions. As I've said previously, in the context of higher education it is really important that the students find game-based learning an acceptable way to learn, and that they are convinced that it is an effective and purposeful method (of course, some students may simply be motivated by the fact that it is a game, but this cannot be assumed for all). Another straightforward way to canvas opinion as to acceptability is a quick survey or questionnaire of the student group. An issue may arise if students have not used game-based learning previously, are unaware of what it involves or have misconceptions as to the types of game that you intend to use. When carrying out a survey it is important that you make sure that students understand what it is you intend and the benefits (as well as any potential drawback) – this can be a way both to avoid negative opinions through lack of understanding and to educate students in what they can expect.

In this section I focus on techniques for carrying out evaluations during the development process. Three areas of game design in which I feel it is essential to involve the user are playability, functionality and usability. Playability considers how well the game works as a game, whether it is fun and enjoyable to play, whether it makes sense to the user and is consistent, whether it is set at the correct level and easy to get started and become engaged in. Functionality looks at aspects such as whether the game does what the users want (or expect) it to and the controls and actions that are available. Usability considers aspects such as whether the controls are logical and consistent, and whether the game is easy to use (as opposed to easy to complete) and interact with.

User-centred design can be seen as an iterative process with a cycle of development and evaluation, with modifications being made at each stage on the basis of user feedback. Prototyping is an important aspect of design and it could be the case that you go through many cycles of iteration before your game is complete. The types of evaluation that you use at different stages of design will differ – for example, it is common to create paper prototypes at an early stage so that feedback can be elicited from users before too much time has been spent on programming and actual development. There are a whole variety of different evaluation techniques you can use and I am only going to cover some of the more common methods here. Any book on interaction design will be able to provide a great deal more detail on method and implementation, but I hope here to provide you with some ideas of ways in which you can ensure that your game is as good as possible.

Paper Prototyping

You can get user feedback early on in the development process, before too much investment has been put into actually building the game, by using paper prototypes or mock-ups of the actual game. For example, to test playability you can ask users to work through any puzzles or challenges in the game to gauge the appropriate level or look at paper versions of screen designs.

Wizard of Oz Prototyping

This type of prototyping is again useful early on in the development process when all the more complex coding work is not necessarily complete. It involves simulating the behaviour of the game, often manually, in a way that is not apparent to the user – from his or her point of view the game is fully functional. An example of the use of the Wizard of Oz method would be a prototype that uses character dialogue generated by a human rather than a complex algorithm.

Scenarios

Asking students to develop or comment on scenarios of use, descriptions of the game and how it might be used and the types of activities that would occur in it can help you gain insights early on into the acceptability of the game, potential shortcomings or problems and ways in which the users might interact with it. Developing scenarios from different user perspectives is also a good way for you to think through the different ways in which students might engage with a game.

Expert Walkthroughs

This involves someone who has a background and expertise in interface design or game design using your game and providing feedback from the point of view of an expert. This can be a very useful technique for highlighting issues and also for getting advice on how they might be resolved.

Think-Aloud Walkthroughs

This involves asking users to interact with the game and talk through what they are thinking so that you can observe how their interaction with the game relates to their thought process. Walkthroughs can be structured so that students have to follow tasks in a specific order or more free form so that you can just see how they go about using the game. This is a good way of highlighting issues with playability or usability of the interface that developers may not recognize because they are so familiar with the system. It is also a good way of evaluating whether students are learning what you expect (or hope) they will learn from playing the game.

Observations

Simply watching people play a game and seeing how they approach tasks and interact with the system will provide you with many insights about what works well and where problems exist. This can be done in person or through the use of video (either recorded or live).

Interviews/Focus Groups

Talking to individuals or groups about their experiences using the game will provide invaluable feedback and enable you to find and address issues where they exist. It also provides a good opportunity to look for creative solutions for problems and to get additional ideas and input from users.

Piloting

Running through the whole game with a small number of users in advance of the real usage will allow you to identify and address any final issues with the game design on a small scale before it is used for real.

You do not need to use huge numbers of students to make user testing worthwhile, which is helpful as it is often difficult to persuade students to take part in evaluations (even with a monetary incentive). I would recommend carrying out evaluations with around four to six users at each stage. This will give you valuable input into the game design without becoming overwhelming or unmanageable.

The amount of user testing that takes place during game development will depend on a number of factors including time and resources available, the type of game being developed and access to willing users to take part in evaluations. There are also heuristic methods that you can use to evaluate games based on established good practice. In the following section I will look at ways to evaluate games for their learning potential, usability and accessibility.

Here and throughout this chapter I use a game I developed as an example of the different types of evaluation that can be implemented during the testing phase, even on a small-scale project. This game, the *Pharaoh's Tomb*, like the *Time Capsule* mentioned previously, was designed to teach basic collaboration and group skills. It was designed for three players who had to work together in a virtual environment in order to solve puzzles and complete the game (see Figure 10.1).

In order to complete the game, players had to be able to navigate through the virtual environment, pick up and drop objects, use objects together and on the

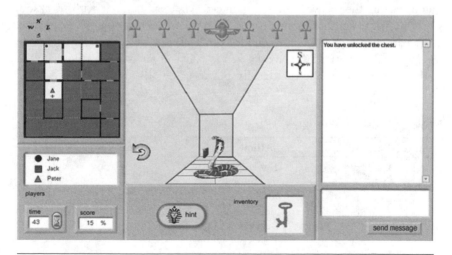

Figure 10.1 The *Pharaoh's Tomb*

environment (e.g. filling up a bucket of water and using it to put out a fire) and talk to other players. There were three phases of user testing that took place, the first focusing on game play, the second on functionality and the third on the usability of the interface. Table 10.1 shows the user testing plan.

The first stage evaluation of game play examined whether the puzzles were logical, solvable, of an appropriate difficulty for the time allowed, and what instructions and hints would be required. The first game prototype offered only basic functionality and several of the puzzles had to be solved on paper; the in-game chat-based communication was not functional at this stage so players had to communicate by talking to one another. This meant that I could watch players collaboratively solve the puzzles to see how they approached them. Players' comments, as well as my observations of their interactions in the gaming environment, were noted throughout the game play and used as a basis for further discussion during a debriefing focus group at the end of the game session.

The second stage of evaluation used a fully functioning prototype to test whether the functionality provided in terms of navigation, interaction, communication and instruction was appropriate and sufficient. In each trial, players were asked to communicate with the other players using only the chat facility but they could ask questions or make comments to the researcher who was observing the session. At the end of the session there was an opportunity for each group to debrief and, in addition, the transcripts from the chat facility in each game session were reviewed to highlight any additional issues.

The final stage of the evaluations, focused on usability and interface design, to refine the user interface and the tools that enable players to navigate, communicate, manipulate objects and solve the puzzles in the game. This set of evaluations was carried out with participants individually, with myself sitting alongside as they played, and a volunteer, who was familiar with the game and located in another room, playing the parts of the two other game players. The participant was not aware that the other players were played by the same person at this stage. Players were asked to play the game, interacting with the other 'players' using the chat facility, but to talk aloud through their actions

Table 10.1 User Testing Plan for the *Pharaoh's Tomb*

Stage	Purpose	Method	Number of participants
1	Game play	Think-aloud walkthrough Debriefing focus group	6
2	Functionality	Observation Debriefing focus group Transcript analysis	10
3	Interface usability	Think-aloud Wizard-of-Oz walkthroughs	4

and thought processes as they did so, making comments on the game itself or on the interface and explaining their chain of thought and the rationale for their actions, which gave the opportunity to clarify, question or probe at the appropriate time.

Activity: Creating a User Testing Plan

It is useful to plan a series of user evaluations into the development process in advance at different stages (you can always add more later if required).

Using the evaluation plan grid from the *Pharaoh's Tomb*, and thinking back to your own game specification, what types of user evaluation would be useful for ensuring that the game is playable, has the correct functionality and is usable?

The process of developing a user evaluation plan early on is helpful because it allows you to build realistic time into the development process for testing, feedback and refinement. It has the additional advantage that it brings to prominence the role and importance of the user in the game development process. As well as ongoing user evaluation during development, which should help you to develop a game that is fit-for-purpose, you can also carry out evaluations during the time that the game is in use and at the end, and there are a number of diagnostic evaluations that you can carry out for yourself based on good practice; I will discuss some of these in the following section.

Evaluating Digital Games

The first question to ask yourself, in terms of evaluation, is exactly what you want to evaluate and why. For example, is the purpose of the evaluation to improve practice, answer a specific question or provide evidence of the effectiveness of the game? Being clear as to the purpose will help to focus the evaluation activity from the start and if there is no purpose to the evaluation this may lead you to consider whether it is worth carrying out in the first place. Some things are easier to evaluate than others, for example, it may be easy to get an idea of whether students find a game to be an enjoyable experience, but more difficult to find out if they have actually learned anything from it – or, in particular, if they have learned what you intended them to learn. Another question to consider is when to evaluate. For example, it may be easier to access students immediately after a teaching session but they may not appreciate the value of using the game until they come to apply the principles learned in practice many months later.

When designing an evaluation I find it very helpful to think at the start about exactly what it is I am trying to evaluate, and write evaluation aims and a data gathering and analysis plan before the game is actually used. Having an evaluation plan is, I think, very important to ensure that you are actually evaluating what you intended and not simply providing a post-hoc rationalization for what was easy to evaluate, or overemphasizing particular areas of the evaluation.

Although anecdotal evidence may not be appropriate in true research, informal feedback from students is an excellent way to gauge how effective they feel a game has been for learning and how much they value it. Be careful though how much stock you put in the opinions of one or two more vocal members of a class, as their opinions may not be representative of the class as a whole and it will be generally those who are least happy that are first to make their opinions known.

There are a number of different types of evaluation that can be undertaken when examining teaching and learning in general and the use of digital games in particular. In Chapter 7 I have already discussed ways of assessing the learning that has taken place using digital games, so I won't dwell on that here. The three areas of evaluation that I am going to look at in this chapter are diagnostic, formative and summative, focusing heavily on diagnostic because I have already discussed techniques for evaluating the student experience with games. Diagnostic evaluation occurs before the activity takes place and involves evaluating aspects such as course design, constructive alignment and the usability and accessibility of the game itself. Formative evaluation involves evaluative activities that take place during the activity and can be used to feed back and inform its use, with the aim of making improvements during the activity. Summative evaluation takes place at the end of the activity and aims to look at the effectiveness of the intervention with hindsight. The areas that formative and summative evaluation examine are broadly similar (it is the timing and purpose of the evaluation that indicates whether it is formative or summative) and may include aspects such as the learning achieved from the game and the student experience.

Diagnostic evaluation is evaluation that takes place before the game activity is used with students. It is carried out in order to identify any previously unrecognized problems and make improvements before the actual implementation. There are a number of ways in which diagnostic evaluations can be carried out, for example, undertaking a systematic review by yourself, or others, using structured checklists or guidelines, having the game reviewed by an expert in the area under review (e.g. course design, interface design) who has not previously seen the game, which has the advantage of bringing an external perspective.

There are two areas in particular where I think that diagnostic evaluation is useful in the context of digital game-based learning, which I will discuss in more detail here. These are the overall accessibility of the game, and the usability of the gaming environment. Undertaking evaluation of accessibility and usability of any games before they are used in a real teaching and learning context provides the opportunity to identify and resolve issues in advance, make modifications and design additional activities to ensure that the game-based learning package is of the highest possible quality.

Accessibility

Accessibility refers to the way in which all students, but in particular those with disabilities, can gain access to and use the gaming environment provided. Diagnostic evaluation can help to ensure that all students have a fair and equal access to the game and that you make any reasonable adjustments or modifications to ensure that the environment is as accessible as possible. Thinking about accessibility will help you make sure (as far a possible) that students with a range of disabilities (e.g. visual or hearing impairments, mobility or cognitive disabilities) will be able to use and be included in the learning experience. This requirement does not only refer to the use of games in learning but actually should be considered for all learning experiences; I mention accessibility here with particular reference to games because of their use of digital technologies and to highlight the fact that it cannot be assumed that all students will have equal access. It is also worth pointing out that in an educational context a consideration of accessibility is required by law (the Disability Discrimination Act in the UK and Section 508 of the Rehabilitation Act in the US).

The degree to which you can ensure universal accessibility will depend to some degree on the development environment in which the game is produced. You may have no influence on the accessibility of commercial games and have to think creatively of ways to ensure that all students have an equivalent experience (the important word here is equivalent, not identical). Different development toolkits will have different levels of accessibility support built in and I would recommend reading up on ways to ensure accessibility as far as possible for the tool you intend to use. The general guidance here is based around guidelines for web accessibility and may be implemented in various ways in different development environments.

As far as possible, textual equivalents should be provided for all auditory and visual content. This will enable players who are accessing the game through a variety of assistive technologies (e.g. screen readers) to access all content. In practice, this may be difficult to achieve without undermining some of the playability of the game, for example when developing an alternate reality game that relies on puzzle challenges of different types we found it impossible to provide an alternative to some of the graphical and auditory puzzles that didn't make the answer obvious to players. In this circumstance we decided that it was important to ensure the integrity and playability of the game and that collaboration would be encouraged to support all players who could not access particular puzzles (which was, in turn, supportive to those who simply could not solve particular puzzles).

Text should be legible, in particular ensuring a reasonable default size and good contrast between foreground and background. The ability to resize text and customize colours will enable users to set their own preferences. Colour combinations with low contrast, particularly those that colour-blind players may not be able to see, need to be avoided, as does the provision of information that relies on colour alone (e.g. a status control that uses red or green as a positive or negative indicator would be inaccessible to people with certain types of colour blindness). Flashing or blinking text or other interface elements should also be avoided.

It is also important to be aware that if you are using an environment that requires the user to navigate through a virtual world – particularly a three-dimensional world – there may be issues of navigation with some users unable to move around, which will negatively affect the overall experience. Additional support and navigational aids (e.g. maps, overlays, alternative views and ways of moving around) should be provided wherever possible. Provision of flexible alternative (and ideally customizable) ways in which to navigate the game and interact with it is good practice. Input methods and devices should be as flexible as possible, for example customization of keyboard input required for movement around a virtual environment.

Unless it is absolutely critical to the learning outcomes, activities that require hand–eye coordination or twitch activities should be avoided, and activities should not be based on achieving a certain objective within a specific time-frame (e.g. completing a mini-game in two minutes), again, unless it is essential for the learning outcomes. See the accessibility checklist.

Accessibility checklist

Textual equivalents provided for all non-textual information?	☐
Default text is legible?	☐
Text size and colours customizable?	☐
Use of colour appropriate?	☐
No flashing elements?	☐
Tools to support navigation?	☐
Alternative methods of navigation and interaction?	☐
No gratuitous requirement for hand–eye coordination?	☐
No gratuitous time limitations?	☐

These guidelines are not comprehensive and an excellent resource on accessibility in education is provided by JISC TechDis at www.techdis.ac.uk. The Accessibility in Learning Guidelines are a good starting point for thinking about the more general issues and how they might apply to a game-based learning experience: http://excellence.qia.org.uk/page.aspx?o=jisctechdis

Unless you have created a game from scratch, it may not be possible to implement some of these points within the gaming environment itself. It is then up to you to decide how big a potential impact any accessibility issues might have and how you plan to address them outside of the gaming environment. Therefore it is important to look at the learning objectives and provide equivalent activities that could support the achievement of those objectives, which could be used or accessed by students who might be unable to make full use of the game itself (e.g. by working in pairs). Legislation (in both the UK and US as well as many other countries) is now clear that it is up to an educational institution to ensure that students with disabilities receive an equivalent educational experience – in all aspects, not just the use of games or in teaching – and have to make reasonable pre-emptive adjustments to make sure that this happens. In practice, this means considering the impact that use of the game could have for a student with a disability and thinking creatively about ways to enable all students to participate. Designing a game where students are required to communicate or work in pairs not only supports collaborative learning but allows students to help each other with areas of difficulty of access. Inclusivity of access is a vital consideration and it is important that you consider the impact of the game in terms of access and to make it as accessible as possible for all – accessible design is good practice and will make the game more usable for all students.

Usability

Usability refers to how easy the gaming software is to learn, interact with and navigate. Benyon *et al.* (2005) describe a computer system that has a high level of usability as being one that is efficient and requires an appropriate amount of effort, effective in that it has appropriate functionality and information organized appropriately, is easy to learn, safe to operate, and has a high level of utility. Usability considers issues such as how effective interaction is, how easy the game is to use, how flexible modes of interaction are and how acceptable it is to students.

In terms of the usability of game-based learning environments, as well as the set of criteria to support educational design, which are described in Chapter 6, a second set emerged from my research that related to the interface design of game-based learning applications. This second set of six criteria examines whether the user interface, elements used and interaction models facilitate learning.

- The environment should allow for *flexible interaction* by the users, where there is a range of different methods of interaction available (e.g. keyboard and mouse), interaction is purposeful in the context of learning not just there for its own sake, controls in the interface are logical and consistent, feedback from the interface on the result of an action is timely and meaningful, and a range of performance indicators are built in (e.g. scores, timers) to enable students to measure their progress and to provide ongoing formative feedback.
- The game should provide *support for player community*, which may be within the game itself or external to the game, e.g. in the form of supporting web resources or forums. Use of avatars (or other ways in which the players can represent themselves) and integrated communication tools can support this, and functionality to support self-regulation of the community, such as moderation, polling or reporting of inappropriate behaviour is useful.
- The interface should provide *transparent navigation* that is clear and consistent and helps the users to move around the environment as well as providing an overview of the player's location (e.g. a map). Help functionality should be obvious and, ideally, alternative methods of navigation should be available.
- The game should provide as much *user control* as possible, so that there are options for customization, the pace and level of play is adjustable and tasks can be undertaken in any sequence. The functionality that the interface provides needs to be appropriate and obvious and instructions should be clear and explicit.
- The game system must be *robust* and allow the users to recover quickly from errors (or not make errors in the first place) and be *responsive* to input so that a player's action will result in a game reaction. Ideally, context-sensitive help and hints should be available and the ability to save the position in the game and return to it at a later stage provided.
- The game environment should have *appropriate visual design* that is – as far as possible – simple, uncluttered and aesthetically pleasing, with text legible, and with the consistent placement of interactive features between screens. Content and information should be available in easily accessible chunks and graphics and rich media should be purposeful rather than unnecessary or distracting.

While these guidelines provide an overview of what is good practice, there will undoubtedly be examples of effective educational games that do not meet one or more of these criteria. Like the guidelines described in Chapter 6, these should be seen as flexible rather than a set of rules that must be adhered to – the pragmatics of digital games for learning mean that the perfect educational game with the perfect interface is unlikely to exist. It is up to you to weigh up how important any failings in terms of these guidelines are in relation to the particular context.

Activity: Evaluating the Usability of Games

Using the usability guidelines described above carry out a review of one of the three games that are described in the introductory chapter of this book.

- Does it provide flexible ways of interacting?
- Is there a player community supporting the game?
- Is navigation of the interface and game world clear and consistent?
- To what degree are you able to control and customize the interface?
- Are you able to recover quickly from errors?
- Is the game responsive to your input?
- Do you think the visual design is appropriate?

Hopefully by undertaking this activity you will have seen that there are a range of usability issues to be addressed when designing games, and not every game will address every one. It is important to note that, though each of these three games has been designed primarily for entertainment, not learning, the guidelines for good usability still apply to a large extent. In practice, when you are developing your own games you may find that one or more of the guidelines are not met and it is then up to you to decide how important you feel the deficiency to be and whether it can be addressed through some other means outside of the game. These guidelines are intended to be a support to the development process, not a straitjacket.

In this final chapter of the technology part of the book I have looked at ways to ensure that any game you produce is as usable as possible for your students. While I have not covered technological implementation in detail (there are plenty of other books that do that) I hope that at this stage you will have a good idea of the different ways of acquiring a game for learning and know how to go about actually finding or building the one you need, and that you have the knowledge to ensure that it is appropriate for your own learning context, fit for purpose and usable by your students.

Chapter Summary

In this chapter I have looked at different ways in which to evaluate digital games for learning. The chapter starts with a discussion of user-centred design and suggests a number of techniques for gaining feedback from users during game development. Suggested techniques were paper prototyping, Wizard of Oz prototyping, scenarios, expert walkthroughs, think-aloud walkthroughs, observations, interviews/focus groups and piloting.

The second part of the chapter looked at the differences between diagnostic, formative and summative evaluations and presented guidelines for ensuring accessibility in games for learning. Finally, the chapter concluded by discussing six guidelines for usability in digital games for learning: flexible interaction, support for player community, transparent navigation, user control, robustness and responsiveness, and appropriate visual design.

Further Reading

D. Benyon, P. Turner & S. Turner (2005). *Designing Interactive Systems*. Harlow: Addison-Wesley. An excellent overview of all aspects of user-centred design.

J. Harvey (Ed.) (1998). *Evaluation Cookbook*. Edinburgh: Heriot-Watt University (retrieved on Jan. 2009 from http://www.icbl.hw.ac.uk/ltdi/cookbook/cookbook.pdf). A wide range of useful ideas for evaluating online learning, much of which are applicable to game-based learning.

CHAPTER 11

Case Studies

This chapter contains six case studies that have been contributed by experienced practitioners in higher education, who have been working with digital games to support learning. Each study presents a discussion of the pragmatics of implementing digital games, looking at the pedagogic rationale, practicalities, technical development and impact of the game.

I hope that these case studies will give you a flavour of the real-life issues that arise when using digital games in real higher education settings, as well as providing evidence that they can be an effective tool to support teaching and learning in this context.

Case Study 1: *Who is Herring Hale?*

Katie Piatt, University of Brighton

The University of Brighton was looking at non-traditional ways to support students' induction, and games were seen as a likely candidate to improve engagement. Alternate reality games were identified as a way to offset the cost and accessibility issues of development, by using familiar, established web technologies and enabling game design to make use of existing physical and virtual resources on and around the University campus.

Any student could play, but direct invitations to the game were sent only to new students who had scored at least 70 per cent on a new students quiz (217 students out of approximately 5,000 new students). The content was designed to allow in-depth and physical exploration of selected support services and resources. In total 42 students completed at least one task in the game (15 per cent of those invited). Twelve students (29 per cent of all active players) completed all ten tasks.

The game took place in Term 1 of the Academic Year 2006/7 and was called *Who is Herring Hale?* The format was a series of ten tasks, one per week over the term, with an underlying time-travel storyline and a supporting online community on the campus social network. The tasks were based on services available to students, both online and in the physical locations around the campus sites.

Delivery of the game was managed through weekly emails that were sent from the Education Detective to players, i.e. those who had completed at least one task or had registered on the supporting community. The emails directed the players to the community area (implemented in a social networking platform) for more information. The support area, blog posts and all printed materials were clearly branded with an orange background and 'h' logo to help players identify with the game and recognize elements when they came across them. Emails triggering the tasks and student responses to the tasks were handled via a dedicated Education Detective email address and managed by the project team.

Each task covered one of the major support services at the University, and was designed to feature an aspect of the service that was felt to benefit from additional highlighting. The clues all involved finding codes and cryptic content that were hidden within normal information about the featured service. The ten tasks and timeline for the game were agreed with the support departments as shown in Table 11.1. Mini-prizes were also available in some weeks.

Design and development of the game involved a range of interested parties from across the University's support departments to submit ideas for their week's clue and work with the game organizer. Delivery of the game involved primarily one member of staff in the Learning Technologies Group to coordinate players, release clues and respond to messages via email and on the community site. This task took some time each day but was estimated to be approximately two hours a day while the game was live. Had player figures been higher an automated system would have been required or more staff involvement. It should be noted that once a task was released it was self-supported by the players. Players for the game were primarily first years, but the game was playable by any student or staff member.

There was no assessment involved for the game players. All of the final 12 players were invited for debriefing (an informal interview) for evaluation purposes and to hand over prizes. Eight interviews took place. Students were observed to fully engage with the quest, and to go as far as offering hints to fellow players in a style befitting the original quest.

This game provided some evidence that the alternate reality game/treasure-hunt format can provide an interesting alternative to existing mechanisms for

Table 11.1 Breakdown of Weekly Activities for *Who is Herring Hale?*

Week	Activity	Prize	Department
Game Week 0	New Student Quiz (open to all new students).	Two iPods	General
Game Task 1	Locate a desk loan book and find a specific name.		Library
Game Task 2	Find and apply for a specific job .		Careers
Game Task 3	Decode a clue hidden in the Meals Vouchers leaflet.	Free coffee voucher sent to all players	Catering
Game Task 4	Decode a message handed out by computer room helpers.	£5 print credit to first 50 to complete. Notebook with clue.	Computing
Game Task 5	Register on the UBSU website and complete a Sudoku puzzle.		Students' Union
Game Task 6	Spot clues hidden in the Fire Safety Video.	Free smoke alarm to first 20 to complete.	Health & Safety
Game Task 7	Reflect on their first term's study in the Good Study Guide blog.	Baseball cap given to everyone who blogged (containing clue).	Study Support
Game Task 8	Find information placed in the Look After Yourself section of Student Services and on Posters.		Student Services
Game Task 9	View a video and collaborate to take photos and load on Community.		General
Last week of term	Debriefing, main prize distribution, evaluation.		

introducing students to certain types of information or services. This format does not appeal to all students, but is very effective for those that like it. The format also provides students with something special to feel part of and to provide a break from their formal courses. The use of a blogging platform for supporting the players was practical and effective.

Sample feedback from the 12 students who completed all tasks:

> In induction week they tell you where to go to get help, Careers for instance. But you forget it all 5 minutes after you've left. This was brilliant – now I really know where to go.

> I was wrapped up in too much programming, it helped give me a break and get a new perspective.

> a really good way to learn

> Thank you all for a wonderful and inspiring term! From chasing orange techie people to strapping spoons on my forehead, it's been fun :)

Several students commented on the feeling of 'fun' and 'being part of something special' and many were clearly deeply immersed in the game. It would be hoped that this could be built on and possibly linked to student retention as a key issue in higher education. One of the factors identified as affecting retention is the quality of the induction process and this model may be able to appeal to an increasingly diverse student population.

The launch of the game coincided with the launch of the University of Brighton's campus-wide social networking system. This provided an easy way for players to collaborate online, and also helped raise awareness of the new system with students, as at that time usage within an academic context within courses was very low. During the first few tasks, it became clear that players were comfortable making use of the community area to help each other and discuss tasks. The game also made use of other existing technologies around the University: quizzes and information on the student Managed Learning Environment, the video streaming service and email. There was a budget of £1000, all of which was spent on prizes: four iPods for the top scorers and memory sticks for the runners up.

No test of the game as a whole was completed. It was always intended to evolve as it was played, taking into account the success of the previous task to gauge the players' readiness for harder tasks or collaboration opportunities. This approach also allowed tasks to be very responsive to real events – such as using information on a new series of posters for a student ball to provide clues for a task, or helping to promote the newly released fire safety video by attracting the players to it. Tests were run by willing colleagues on each weekly task just prior to release to check instructions were clear.

Tips

- Don't be disappointed by low take-up – mysteries and puzzles just don't appeal to everyone.
- Make any scoring completely fair and transparent to avoid criticisms.
- Provide a way for the students to share and collaborate on tasks.

Case Study 2: *Marketplace*

Niki Hynes, Strathclyde University
Nicola Whitton, Manchester Metropolitan University

The *MarketPlace* business game was used as a core part of a collaborative, final-year undergraduate marketing course, Marketing Management in Practice, at Napier University in Edinburgh. *Marketplace* (see Figure 11.1) provides an online virtual business environment, in which groups of students work as companies to compete against one another for market share and position. Activities involve undertaking market analysis, designing marketing strategies

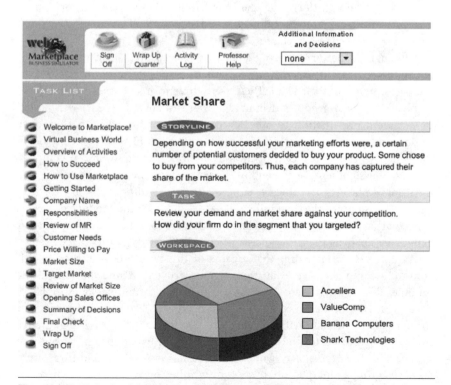

Figure 11.1 The *Marketplace* Online Game (image reproduced with permission of Innovative Learning Solutions, Inc.)

and designing appropriate product mixes for development. The game aims to teach the application of marketing skills within a real-world context. The game-based course was piloted during the academic session 2004/5 and 42 students elected to study on the module.

The game was played for the whole semester in which the course ran and was at the heart of all activities. At the start of the course, students were split into teams, or virtual companies, of four or five members and were expected to work within those teams for the duration. The course was 15 weeks in total and within that time the game was broken down into eight decision periods, during which groups had to make decisions about the company, its marketing strategies and the products it wanted to develop. Although *Marketplace* is an online game and decisions are input online, students were expected to meet face-to-face to discuss decisions, and one person would update the company profile at the end of each decision period. At the end of the period, the simulation game provided immediate feedback and showed the performance of companies relative to one another within the virtual environment.

Classes for the course consisted of lectures and tutorials, with five lectures in total and a three-hour tutorial slot each week in which students were expected to make their group decisions (although they were also able to meet outside the allocated tutorial slot). Attendance at the tutorial was compulsory, and a tutorial worksheet had to be completed and signed by all group members and handed in at the end of each tutorial.

Although the performance of each team was measured against that of other teams to provide a competitive environment, students were not assessed on the performance of their team. There were three forms of assessment, split in emphasis between group and individual performance. Students were asked to prepare a presentation to the 'Board of Directors' on their performance to date and future plans, which took place after the fifth decision period of the game (worth 40 per cent of the final mark). They also had to complete individual assignments at the end of the simulation (worth 40 per cent), and the team worksheets detailing decisions made in each tutorial period (worth 20 per cent). As part of the final individual assessment for the module, as well as their analysis of the marketing aspects, students were asked to reflect on their experiences playing the game and working collaboratively with others.

As this was the first time that a game of this type had been used in this context, a comprehensive evaluation was undertaken. Before the start of the module, the students were asked to complete an attitudinal questionnaire, covering their attitudes to computer game-playing and educational games. For the formative and summative evaluations, both qualitative and quantitative measures were used to find out about the student experience of learning in groups with the *Marketplace* game. The module was evaluated in three ways: six focus groups took place halfway through the course; students were asked to complete an attitudinal questionnaire at the end of the module; and the reflective statements on the student learning experiences within the game (a mandatory part of the final assessment) were analysed.

The focus groups took place between weeks six and eight of the course and in total 20 students took part. Although these focus groups were optional, students who took part were paid a small fee in order to encourage a range of students to take part. Each focus group had three or four students in it and took approximately one hour. Each followed a similar structure but questions were open-ended and were used as an opportunity to explore in any direction that seemed appropriate. Focus groups were used rather than individual interviews because of time constraints and because it was hoped that a group interview would help to stimulate ideas and debate. The group make-up avoided students who were in the same work groups together as it was felt that this might hinder honest discussion of experiences.

The focus groups examined the students' expectations and motivations, work patterns and communication, the course and game design. Data from these groups were used to highlight themes and to design the end-of-course attitudinal questionnaire. This questionnaire was presented to students in the final week of the course and in total 26 students completed and returned it.

The students who took part in the module were final-year students from a range of marketing and business disciplines. They were predominantly aged in their early twenties and approximately two-thirds of the class was female. Most of the class had previous experience of playing computer games but only 12 per cent had used an educational game of any sort before. The vast majority of students (85 per cent) said that using a game to learn would not motivate them either way, positive or negative. The questionnaire feedback provided a positive indication of the overall success of the module, with 80 per cent of students saying that they had enjoyed this module more than others (these data can only be indicative as only 60 per cent of the class responded to the final questionnaire).

The students who elected to study this course did not do so primarily because it was a game, but because it was novel and because it sounded fun and interesting. Other common motivations for undertaking the course were because it was continually assessed with no final examination and because it offered the opportunity to apply theory to a real-life situation. When asked if they were motivated to do well in the module, 96 per cent of the students said that they were. In contrast, 77 per cent said that they were motivated to do well in the game. It seemed that motivation to win the game changed throughout the playing period depending on the performance of the team, with winning teams becoming more motivated while groups who were performing less well quickly lost their motivation. There was a large amount of competition between groups, but not among individual members of groups, and this appeared to be a positive motivation, but again more so for teams that were performing better.

The evaluation also highlighted positive and negative aspects of a game-based approach. Students liked the fact that feedback from each decision was provided immediately, however they also felt that the feedback was limited and that it did not explain exactly why actions had led to certain consequences. The game was also criticized for not always seeming to reflect the correct application of theory and for the fact that it would be possible to win by chance. It was also felt that the game was based on a very limited model with limited options and that there was no potential within the game for creativity or expression of individual talent.

Tips

- You do not have to stick to the structure provided by the game, but can add in additional creative elements.
- Encourage intra-group competition to motivate students while still supporting collaboration.
- Do not assess game performance directly.

Case Study 3: *PeaceMaker*

Chris Goldsmith and Richard Hall, De Montfort University

Up to 24 final-year undergraduate students studying politics and/or international relations at De Montfort University can take an optional module on 'Ethics and International Relations in the Middle East'. The interplay between ethical concerns and international politics has become more pronounced in recent years in both the theoretical and practical aspects of politics, as evidenced by the debates surrounding the UK Labour Government's idea of making explicit an ethical dimension in foreign policy. During the module students debate and discuss issues like: the promotion of democracy in non-democratic states; global inequality; Just War theories; conflict resolution; and the politics of identity and difference.

In order to support the students' recognition of how these theories impact in practice, they are exposed to a series of case studies on politics in the Middle East, including: the Arab–Israeli conflict; the Gulf War 1990–1; the invasion and occupation of Iraq 2003–8; and the rise and fall of the Oslo Peace Process. In order to underpin the pedagogy of the module, students play *PeaceMaker*, a commercial digital game which requires them to take on the role of either the Israeli Prime Minister or Palestinian President. Each player's objective in the game is to achieve a solution to the Israeli–Palestinian dispute.

The subject teaching team has considerable experience in using simulations and role-playing exercises in the teaching of politics and international relations. Drawing on the work of educationalists like John Dewey, Paulo Freire and David Kolb, the curriculum has been designed to combine experiential learning opportunities with more traditional delivery. Throughout the three years of the degree programme students are regularly required to apply their knowledge and skills to real-world situations. For example, during the second-year module on the 'Politics of the European Union' students spend up to three months participating in a simulation of negotiations in the Council of Ministers. For much of this time they work together developing policy positions, responding to 'news' stories and conducting pre-meeting talks via the virtual learning environment. The simulation concludes with a day-long negotiation session where the delegations meet face-to-face. Students gain an in-depth appreciation of the dynamics of EU negotiations as well as developing their negotiation, public speaking and listening skills.

Consequently when we came to designing the 'Ethics and International Relations in the Middle East' module, the question of including a further simulation element was at the forefront of our minds. However, there was some reticence about this due to the highly charged nature of the subject matter. Students tend to be passionate advocates for one side or the other on the Israeli–Palestinian question, which can lead to confrontation in the classroom. Therefore, key learning outcomes for the learners were to appreciate the complexity of the issues that are faced in the region, to raise their awareness of how those issues are perceived differently by both sides and to develop some understanding of the challenges of the process of conflict resolution. The challenge was how to enable students to do this in an inclusive and scholarly way rather than remaining entrenched in their preconceived political positions. An approach to active learning within collaborative settings, focused around real-time decision-making, was crucial. The *PeaceMaker* game offered a potential way to achieve this, as students could experience the peace process from both sides of the conflict in a controlled manner. This provided an opportunity that would be much more complex and time-consuming in a more traditional simulation.

The teaching team's awareness of using digital games in teaching had been raised by workshops that focused discussion on game-playing as a means of engaging students. It took a full year to develop a pedagogic rationale for games-based approaches that would focus upon how digital and non-digital games might be integrated and delivered. The work of Weir and Baranowski (2008) on using the commercial game *Civilization* in introductory international relations classes was insightful in highlighting the practice-based design issues.

The first of these was the critical importance of narrative frameworks and providing students with a context for the game before playing it. This would inform the timescale for the game and what the team would expect the students to learn from it. If students had already received lectures on the Arab–Israeli conflict and the Middle East Peace Process before they played the game, it was possible that they might treat the game play more as a re-enactment than an experience. Part of the pleasure of playing is experimentation without fear of punishment (or in this case of being wrong, making poor decisions or failure to resolve conflict). If the student had a sense of behaving ahistorically, they might feel constrained in their in-game choices. However, playing the game without some prior briefing of the issues might mean that players found it hard to understand the meaning of their actions. Within the game there is a historical timeline that provides a basic overview of the development of the Israeli–Palestinian debate. Students who used it during a trial session found it useful, but others had not even noticed that the option was available. The team chose to use the game before the students had had specific inputs about the Middle East peace process, but they were clearly advised in the instructions to consult the timeline before beginning the game.

Secondly, we had to consider how we were going to structure the actual gaming sessions. Although *PeaceMaker* cost less than £10 at the time due to the favorable exchange rate, we did not believe that students would pay that much to install the game on their own computers. As a consequence we installed the game on ten computers in a Humanities Faculty Computing Lab. This had the advantage of easily available technical support if anything went wrong, alongside the ability to monitor progress and deal with student queries. However, these rooms are heavily booked throughout the week, so dedicated gaming sessions had to be short, up to one hour in duration, and this impacted on the students' sense of engagement. In addition, there were problems in resuming saved games due to the configuration of machines over the network.

The teaching team had to design gaming sessions to get the most out of an hour's play. Students were asked to play in pairs: one to do the onscreen work; the other to take notes about options that they had chosen, rationale for their approach and impressions gained from play. In the game it is quite possible to resolve the issues within an hour (at least on the easy level), but even if they did not succeed in completing a game, they could record their score. The students were then asked to play the game in a second session, taking the role of the other, Israeli or Palestinian, leader.

A central issue for the team to consider was how to assess the *PeaceMaker* experience. Simulations have been used as a form of real-time assessment in the past. For example, the EU Council of Ministers simulation, which occurs at level two, forms 30 per cent of the module assessment, based upon a substantial number of individual and group outputs that can be assessed. This simulation has the following elements:

- A day-long assessment, where students are split into groups and asked to devise a negotiating strategy for a series of discussions around a contemporary theme of European integration.

- Simulated discussions have included the draft EU Constitution, negotiations on Croatian and Turkish accession to the Union, and debates on the reform of the Common Agricultural Policy.
- The module website is used to set up and prepare each group's strategy, and enables each delegate to post a report on a particular aspect of their group's overall strategy; these are accessible by members of other delegations, and enable students to identify potential negotiating partners or barriers to agreement.
- The reports reflect the permanent representative stage of European Union policy negotiations and form 15 per cent of the overall simulation grade, and submission is an entry criterion to the group marks awarded on the day of the simulation itself. The remaining 85 per cent is based on group performance.

For the *PeaceMaker* simulation the learning outcomes focus upon developing a broader appreciation of Middle East politics and a deeper understanding of the complexities of conflict resolution. Therefore, the team decided not to tie a piece of assessed coursework to the game directly, but to use it for formative evaluation.

Students were asked to reflect on a series of questions and post their reflections within an online learning journal on the virtual learning environment, because that was software with which they were familiar. At level three, developing a reflective approach is central as learners move towards independent study and autonomy. The reflections in the logs provided further evidence for students as they prepared for both assessed seminar presentations and a second essay which specifically focused upon issues that impact decisions made in *PeaceMaker*, namely: the promotion of democracy in non-democratic states; global inequality; Just War theories; conflict resolution; and the politics of identity and difference. Some students dealt with their relative success or failure as peacemakers, some with what they learnt about the issues and others wrote about their feelings about the game. These specific examples of reflection and personal learning through decision-making were then discussed in seminars, and focused within a discussion forum where students had to post a maximum 250-word synopsis.

Feedback showed that the game proved particularly useful in the way that students gained a deeper appreciation of the asymmetries of the specific problem. The strategies that work playing the game as the Israeli Prime Minister are completely impractical when you are Palestinian President, so they began to understand the different pressures on the two sides. Students also demonstrated emotional responses to the game, for example, anger at terrorist acts or Israeli incursions or frustration at the seeming intractability of the problems. This enabled them to gain added insights into the conflict-resolution process. These reflections were then built upon by some students in coursework essays on the subject. Finally some students critiqued the assumptions about the Middle East that were built into the game, particularly the stress on a two-state solution.

Overall, using *PeaceMaker* was a very positive experience for staff and students. Students generally enjoyed playing the game, although some hardened gamers were rather scathing about the graphics, and they certainly appreciated the insights that they gained from looking at the process from both sides. The staff team felt that later discussions about the Israeli–Palestinian problem had been more considered than was previously the case. While student positions on the key issues had not greatly changed, there was more appreciation of the complexity and intractable nature of the problem. This was clearly reflected in coursework on the topic, which was much less polemical than in previous years. The team is now preparing for another run of *PeaceMaker* and looking at the possibility of working digital games into other modules in the curriculum where appropriate.

Tips

- You do not have to reinvent the wheel. There may be an off-the-shelf product that you can use or modify to achieve your learning outcomes. It is often a case of how you frame the activity, in the context of reflective learning and personal ownership of the narrative and processes within a gaming situation.
- Debriefing players is crucial. You need to give students questions to reflect on immediately after the gaming session, which are linked into whole-class or small-group sessions. Specific debriefing sessions connected to written assignments help to focus student evaluation of decision-making and actions.
- You do not always need to tie the game directly to summative assessment. However, activities should be designed to capture formative experiences, and these should be linked explicitly to summative assessment. For instance, learning journals that demonstrate reflection and application of theory to practice help empower students to take ownership of their learning.

Case Study 4: *Red Frontier*

Elisabeth Yaneske, University of Teesside

The idea for my game came about through my experience of teaching programming to computing students at the University of Teesside. I noticed that year after year students learning to program seemed to struggle with the same concepts. I wanted to find a way of helping learners concretize these concepts using visual metaphors and I felt that a game environment would be ideal. The game is aimed at adult learners, primarily students studying in higher education, who are learning to program. The game has been used by 71 computing students.

The game story is based around a crisis on Earth, A virulent fungus is spreading over the arable land and wiping out the Earth's crops. Scientists have not been able to find an effective fungicide and so a decision has been taken to set up biodomes on Mars in order to grow crops to feed the starving billions on Earth. A number of facilities have been set up on Mars but they are not yet operational. The mission of the player is to get the facilities operational so that the biodomes can be built and crops shipped back to Earth. There are three facilities that are not yet operational: the power plant, the seed sorter and the manufacturing plant. The power plant provides power to the whole facility, the manufacturing plant cuts the biodome material into the shapes required for their manufacture, and the seed sorter ensures that only uncontaminated seeds are planted in the biodomes. Each facility requires some programming to get the equipment working. Players use a graphical user interface to create the correct pseudocode to control the equipment in each facility. The name of the game and the facility on Mars is *Red Frontier*.

The design of the game is based on the premise that programming languages share several abstract concepts, such as control structures. These concepts are often harder to understand than the programming syntax itself, especially for those learning their first language. The consequence of not understanding these concepts is poor algorithm design leading to inefficient and non-scalable program code. Unfortunately, when learners test their code they only receive errors when there is a problem with the programming syntax, similar to running a spell check in a word-processing package. In the same way that perfect spelling and grammar do not ensure a prize-winning novel, perfect programming syntax does not ensure a good program. Learners become product-focused rather than process-focused, with their main criterion being whether a program works rather than whether the code is efficient and scalable. Syntax errors can also put students off programming early and make them overly cautious, causing them to make more mistakes. The aim of *Red Frontier* is to help learners concretize abstract programming concepts, such as how a loop works and why it is better to use a loop rather than multiple IF statements, which are generic concepts. The game does not teach program syntax which is program-specific. Players create code by selecting options from a toolbox in a visual programming environment. The advantage of using a game for this purpose is that it can provide an engaging simulation where learners can be presented with problems in context and receive immediate feedback on their actions.

The underlying pedagogy of the game is based on experiential learning theory or 'learning by doing' and on a social constructivist view of learning. The game is played by groups of two to three learners working together as a group to solve each problem. The dialogue between the learners forms an important part of the learning process. Learners have to justify their opinions to the rest of the group in order to have their solution accepted. As mentioned before, one of the advantages of using a game is that it provides instant feedback in context on the player's actions. Players receive hints on problems detected in their solutions. They are able to step through the code and see how the values of variables change. When the players implement a working solution they receive feedback on the design of their solution. The feedback shows them a model answer and tells them explicitly about the advantages of the design. Players are encouraged to reflect on these good design principles once they have finished playing the game.

The player's actions are recorded as a script which can then be played back. This script serves two purposes. The script can be used as a teaching tool to encourage reflection in the group through discussion whilst going through the playback. The script records each keystroke made by the players as well as their mouse movements. In order to understand what the players are actually thinking when they make conceptual mistakes they are asked to talk through the playback explaining what they are doing at each stage. Having a formal method of recording how students program and being able to discuss why they have made certain assumptions allows further misconceptions to be identified. These misconceptions are documented and may lead to the modification of the game to add further puzzles or perhaps the development of further games or other teaching tools to address these issues. Often, if a program compiles and executes without error then a student will assume that that is all that matters. They will rarely ask for feedback on the design of the program. The game gives an opportunity for all students to receive formative feedback on the design of their solutions.

At present the game contains three facilities: the power station, the manufacturing plant and the seed sorter (see Figure 11.2). Each facility has an associated problem that players must solve in order to get the Mars base operational. Players can choose the order in which to solve the problems but are advised that the seed sorter is the easiest problem to solve.

On entering the seed sorter scenario the player will be shown an animation of a checking machine with a red and green light and two tracks exiting the machine. They must program the seed sorter so that contaminated seeds are incinerated to prevent the fungus spreading to Mars. A red light indicates that seeds are contaminated. The track on the left goes to the incinerator. The players must program the track direction based on the light state. This problem acts as an introduction to the game interface but also teaches the players about using

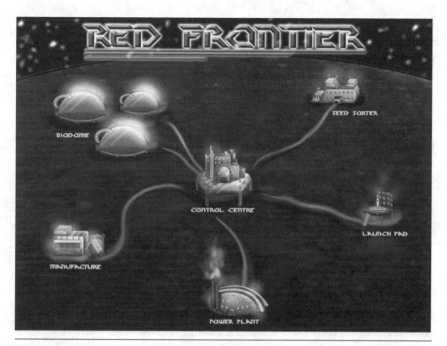

Figure 11.2 *Red Frontier*

a function within a conditional statement. As a general feature for all problems players must initialize variables before using them.

The manufacturing plant shows an animation of a cutting machine that at present does not know how to cut shapes. The intended learning outcome for this task is that learners understand the advantages of a generic function. Players are asked to write a function to cut a square, and then a function to cut a triangle. Then the game explains that rather than have a separate function for each shape it would be more efficient to have a generic function that could cut any regular polygon required. The task for the players is to create this generic function so that the biodomes can be constructed from the cut material.

The power station must periodically check the status of the generators to determine the total power that is being generated and whether any generators are faulty. Players are asked to create a function that accepts a list of generators that are currently on. It is assumed that if the generator is on then it will have a power output greater than zero. Players are therefore told that faulty generators will have a power level of zero. The function must return the total power output from all generators. The desired learning outcome for this puzzle is that learners understand how a FOR EACH loop works to cycle through each element within an array.

With each of these scenarios tasks players are provided with a list of functions that are available for them to use. When they run their code they see an animation that either shows the equipment working successfully or the equipment failing. The animations are important as a visual representation of the task they are trying to solve. This helps learners to visualize the task and relate it to the non-virtual world that they already understand.

Students were asked to play the game during scheduled tutorial time in the computer labs. The game had to be installed on each computer before the session. I was present during these sessions to provide technical help and general support to students. The game had initially been tested with first- and second-year undergraduate students studying programming as part of their degree. The participants were asked to complete an online survey that asked them about the game interface and also their perception of how well the game helped them learn. In addition, focus groups were conducted with student volunteers in order to obtain more qualitative feedback.

In general, students enjoyed playing the game and were engaged in the puzzles. In terms of learning, most students felt that the game had helped them learn by providing a way of applying theory in context. It helped them to visualize the advantages of certain design choices. Feedback from students led to the generation of 'bug lists' that contained a combination of technical problems that the students had uncovered and user interface changes that the students requested. Tutors of the modules involved were keen to use the game again and felt that it added value to the student experience. It is intended to trial the game in more modules and further develop it with more puzzles.

It was decided that the C# programming language should be used for the development of *Red Frontier*. First, C# is ideal for creating user interfaces and handling user interaction via the Forms library. C# is also a good language for rapid development and code maintainability. One downside to C# (and other managed languages) as opposed to a native language like C++ is that it runs slower, however it was not felt that the requirements of *Red Frontier* were such that they would require the extra speed. The application relies on the playback of video which has been created using Flash and then encoded so as to be played back within *Red Frontier* via the standard media player.

Development began with the assembly of a set of requirements. From this a design document was created to be used as an overview during application development. The development phase itself consisted of a number of small iterations adding functionality leading towards fulfilling all the requirements (agile coding method). Once new functionality was in place it was tested as fit for purpose and for any bugs. The final phase was a longer test phase, testing functionality and usability. Each development iteration was concluded with a test phase where functionality and usability were tested. This naturally led to some alterations that were then fed back into the next iteration. Once the application was complete a fuller testing phase was carried out. As well as spotting some further bugs, this helped detect any issues the user may have with the interface.

I applied for funding from the Enterprise Development Fund available at the University of Teesside and obtained £3,000 to develop the game. Half of this money was spent on the development of the game specification and on the game engine and game interface. The other half of the money was used to pay an animator to create the introduction animation for the game, the game map and the failure and success animations for each of the puzzles. The money spent on the animations was a true reflection of the cost but the money spent on development did not in reality cover the developer's time.

Tips

- Think hard about the scope of the game and what is achievable with money, resource and budgetary constraints. Otherwise the game may never get finished.
- Test, test and test again. User-centred design is essential to the success of the game.
- Make your game scalable, include the ability to update the content and add new content.

Case Study 5: *The Retail Game*

John Pal and Mark Stubbs, Manchester Metropolitan University

The Retail Game (www.theRetailGame.com) was designed to be used by first-year undergraduates on the BA (Hons) retail marketing degree at MMU Business School. It replaced a paper-based store-planning exercise where students had to make both strategic and operational decisions about how a new retail outlet should be positioned in a small town (see Figure 11.3).

The game has been used on the 'Retail Operations' unit, a compulsory course for first-year students on the retail marketing degree. The unit is one of six studied in the first year, and students undertake both a piece of coursework assessment and end of year examination. The game has also been used at Babson College in Boston, USA, where final-year students undertake the game as part of a larger unit run by leading retail academic Professor Michael Levy.

The full cohort has used the game; the unit usually enrols about 30 students but the game has also been used with groups of up to 50 international business students on an English-language summer school.

Users are provided with background information about the fictional retail clothing company, FashCo, who currently have 50 outlets of up to 2,000 square

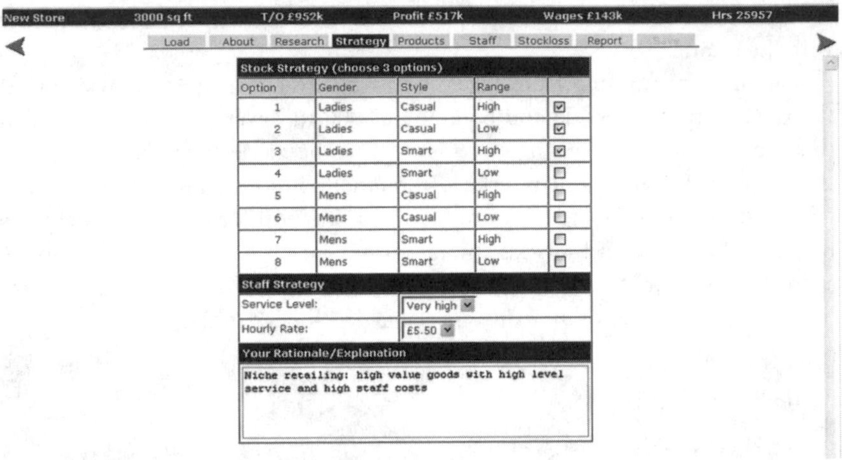

New Store		3000 sq ft		T/O £952k		Profit £517k		Wages £143k		Hrs 25957

Load　About　Research　**Strategy**　Products　Staff　Stockloss　Report

Stock Strategy (choose 3 options)

Option	Gender	Style	Range	
1	Ladies	Casual	High	☑
2	Ladies	Casual	Low	☑
3	Ladies	Smart	High	☑
4	Ladies	Smart	Low	☐
5	Mens	Casual	High	☐
6	Mens	Casual	Low	☐
7	Mens	Smart	High	☐
8	Mens	Smart	Low	☐

Staff Strategy

Service Level:	Very high ▾
Hourly Rate:	£5.50 ▾

Your Rationale/Explanation

Niche retailing: high value goods with high level service and high staff costs

Figure 11.3 *The Retail Game*

feet in size. Allied with this, the introductory background information contains a series of linked pages titled 'Research'. These pages provide data on local competition, national clothing trends and the demographic composition of the local population. Also provided are current performance data for the company as a whole, e.g. sales per square foot by product.

Armed with these data users have to choose and justify a product and service strategy (which incorporates levels of service and wage rates). Having chosen their strategy users are then presented with further screens where they are required to allocate space to products, determine the staffing complement in terms of the proportion of permanent to temporary staff, and the proportion of full-day to part-day staff. Moving through the game users also have to decide upon, and justify, a stockloss prevention strategy before finally being presented with a results page that can be printed off. On the results page is a blank store plan that has to be completed off-screen using the space allocation decisions made earlier in the process.

The previous paper-based exercise with the same learning objectives required too much emphasis on data entry and manipulation, and whilst the use of a spreadsheet template enabled the teaching team to validate results, far too much time was spent in this part of the exercise for both staff and students. In addition, a mis-entry by students could jeopardize their whole proposal. Most critically it was felt that too little understanding of the principles involved in the new store planning process was demonstrated. In order to undertake the exercise groups had to be formed and the issues of non-participation and lack of reflection were clearly evident. By contrast the new approach permitted anytime/anywhere (home or university) flexibility.

Moreover the new approach enabled the testing of various proposals and the iterations undertaken by students allowed them to see the impact of changing variables on their final outcome. By removing the time-consuming data entry and validation process by the adoption of a database-driven exercise, which had conditions that could not be breeched, it was ensured that only fully formed proposals could be submitted.

The overriding concern was to ensure that greater user emphasis was given to the development and justification of underlying principles rather than the tedium of data entry. By adopting a database-driven 'back end' the data could to be changed from year to year with very little effort by the teaching team.

The overarching approach used was that aligned to the Kolb cycle with an emphasis on the testing out of various combinations of product and service mix. The lecture and tutorial programme that ran alongside the students' use of the game enabled them to either start from a theoretical/principles stance or immediately immerse themselves in the frequent testing out of ideas. With user feedback we made a number of fundamental changes: the introduction of a performance toolbar across all screens enabled users to see quickly their planned financial returns; the introduction of mandatory free-text prompts to justify decisions made at each stage ensured that 'click and move' actions were avoided; and a save function was developed so that different proposals could be compared before submitting a chosen one for assessment.

The learning outcomes related to a knowledge base, namely an understanding of marketing principles and retail operational issues, such as an appreciation of store layout principles and labour scheduling requirements; and to decision-making skills and the justification of decisions made. The use of the Chartered Institute of Marketing's asset requirements was also taken account of in the design. Interpersonal skills were tested by the requirement for students to undertake the game on their own and then they formed small groups and submitted one group effort based on their accumulated knowledge from doing the game. As well as the lectures and tutorials that ran alongside the exercise, bespoke tutor feedback on each submission was provided, as was generic feedback.

As already alluded to, the users have to do three main tasks in the game:

- Examine and interpret the research data about the company, local population and national trends.
- Make decisions on store positioning in terms of products to display and the scheduling of the workforce as well as considering their wage rates and composition.
- Justify decisions at each stage through text boxes.

Around the game first-year undergraduate students had to provide a short report outlining the strengths and weaknesses of their proposals as well as drawing on best practice and benchmark data of other retailers. The international summer school cohort delivered an oral presentation about their decisions.

For three years the game was used as the platform for a separate interpersonal skills unit delivered solely to retail-enrolled students. The context of the game, which focuses on the planning of the new store, was embellished and all students were provided with the first year's trading results. In addition each student was provided with a brief description of an executive role, e.g. stockloss prevention manager, finance director, buying director and so on, and certain objectives. Students then met in groups of eight and used their role-play vignettes as a basis for negotiating what should happen to remedy the trading situation.

The game was introduced to students at an oral briefing, although in later years announcements and documents listed in the unit's virtual learning environment was all that was required for students to gain access and get started. Similarly the game has been used at Babson College without any input from the designers of the game – the use of a briefing pack provided to the tutor there sufficed.

The outputs from the game itself provided one measure of students' understanding of the principles involved in the opening of a new store as well as appreciating the practice gained through both decisions made and the justifications of those decisions through the benchmarking activity that students were supposed to engage in.

It was clear that greater appreciation of the principles was achieved and the student feedback was favourable. Both these areas are reported on in our other articles about the game (Pal & Stubbs, 2002; Stubbs & Pal, 2003; Pal *et al.*, 2005).

A web-based browser format was chosen that meant that the game was not reliant on any specific software package. Whilst this gave greater flexibility it meant that the use of active server page technology had to be tested on a whole range of browsers.

One of the team had a half-time release from normal duties through the awarding of a university fellowship. However, too much of that time was spent in the initial stages in trying to master Macromedia Ultra Dev. On securing funds from a European Social Fund Project the novice programmer (John) was able to recruit the technically adept programming skills (of Mark) required for the project to get completed. The costs of about £5,000 did not however show the true costs of programming as the hours logged were far in excess of those claimed.

The design was a collaboration between two individuals with complementary skills: one with the technical savvy to write the appropriate scripting and the other with the retail-specific know-how. A rapid prototyping approach was adopted and once the overarching design was established the greatest amount of the time was given over to testing of the site. There is no doubt that a major part of the time spent on the development of the site was spent on testing the game.

Tips

- Be clear in your objectives.
- Keep objectives simple.
- Be prepared to be frustrated by the technology.
- Enable users to see progress rather than having a black-box approach that many other games tend to use.

Case Study 6: *World of Warcraft*

David White, University of Oxford

World of Warcraft (*WoW*) is a massively multi-player online (MMO) game in which players battle with mythical creatures in a 3D world which is a thematic and aesthetic rendering of the fantasy genre. The phenomenal success of the game and its realization of a Tolkien-style world often mask the sophisticated processes and structures which motivate the players to learn. In many respects this form of gaming is the apex of online social and collaborative spaces. When abstracted away from the slaying of dragons *WoW* foregrounds numerous technical and social principles which can be applied to e-learning more generally.

The core aim of the game in *WoW* is to reach the highest experience level by completing tasks. These start as very simple quests which can be done quickly by an individual player and gradually scale up until in the later stages of the game it requires up to 25 players working as a team hours per session to progress. Players can choose a version of the game in which they can fight each other, fight the environment (computer-generated characters) or simply role-play. The player against environment version is of most interest as the competitive aspect of play is driven by a range of factors all of which are amplified by the game's ability to support a society of players. In a single-player game you are competing solely against the computer (the leader board in traditional arcade games is a notable exception which moves the single-player game to one that is socially competitive); in *WoW* and other MMO games elements such as experience points and game gear (armour, swords, spells, etc.) become embodied forms of social capital. So whilst an individual player's primary focus will be to move up through the levels, their motivation is as much to gain the respect of their in-world peers as it is to complete the game. In addition this social dimension encourages other more complex motivations such as being known as trustworthy or as a good team player.

WoW uses a number of techniques to encourage the formation of communities of players rather than simply having multiple individuals in the same space. The three most significant are their management of presence, the formation of multi-skilled teams and the pursuit of clear goals within an overarching narrative. The first two of these are, in my opinion, areas which have not been properly investigated by those designing online learning spaces or programmes of study.

A crucial factor in harnessing the motivation that can come from being part of a community of learners is gaining the trust of the individuals who take part. They need to know that the environment is safe but they also need to trust that there are other people present in that environment who will react to their contributions in some form. This factor is what motivates participation/communication and is a necessary precursor to cooperation and forms of social constructivist learning. In *WoW* the player is immediately aware of the social presence of others via their realization as avatars (i.e. they can literally see them walking around) and by the general chat channel which is open by default. This chat channel is available to all players. Its movement as individuals contribute is an indication that there are other real people in the environment. These forms of presence are often not explicitly engaged with by the new player but they give an ambient sense of others which builds a feeling of potential community and allows the new player to learn the etiquette and rites of passage of the world without having initially to risk visible engagement. These low-risk forms of presence shift the satisfaction of completing game goals from the personal to the social.

WoW has been designed to encourage the formation of teams. When players choose a character to tackle the game they are selecting a specific range of potential skills such as magic, healing or fighting. In the later stages of the game goals can only be reached by groups of players made up from a range of races and classes to balance out these skills. Each player learns their role within the society of the game as they progress then joins a multi-skilled team in the later stages. The explicit assignment of roles in this manner encourages collaboration and through this collaboration the sense of belonging and worth of an individual within the game world is amplified. The format of the game allows players to experiment with different characters and therefore different roles to find the one they excel at or have the most fun with. The majority of players will have more than one character they can play at any one time depending on the type of role they wish to play in any given session.

In terms of teaching and learning, assigning roles is crucial to collaboration. Often the roles need to evolve within a student group and cannot be made as explicit as within a game. Nevertheless the design of goals which actually require a multi-skilled team rather than simply more person hours than an individual can cope with is often not properly considered when designing online learning.

In some cases making roles more explicit whilst allowing the flexibility to change roles often could aid successful collaborative learning rather than simply working with an expectation that once certain communication tools are provided teamwork will follow. It is certainly the case that shared endeavour is a key factor in the facilitation of communities of learners.

The practice of teaching and learning online should be influenced by the games designers as many techniques both technical and social can be abstracted away from gaming genres which could be effective in the service of e-learning. I am not making a case that all learning should be 'gamed' nor that it is possible to mask subjects in fantasy or science fiction genres. It is simply that many of the challenges that the games designers face in terms of motivation, engagement and learning are similar to those faced by those designing the next generation of e-learning which hopes to take advantage of the expansion of social media tools/spaces on the web.

Tips

- Don't try and teach in *WoW* – the genre and aesthetic is too strong.
- Watch someone playing the game and try to understand what is motivating them.
- If you don't think that social aspects of learning are important don't look at *WoW*.
- The breadth of communication channels and activities from the formal to the informal, from the private to the public, are what makes this game a success. Consider which of these types of channels/activities are needed in the context of your own teaching, bearing in mind that all communities spend much of their time interacting *off-topic*.

CHAPTER **12**
Conclusions

In this final chapter I draw together some of the key points from the previous parts of the book and reflect on the current state of play of digital games for learning in higher education, looking at areas where I think future research would be valuable. This chapter also highlights some of the challenges for learning with digital games and considers key areas for future research.

I hope that by the time you have reached this chapter you have gained an overview of the theoretical context of digital games in higher education and have found my arguments for their use convincing. I hope also that you have generated your own ideas for designing games in your own teaching and learning context and have identified the next steps you need to take in order to make the use of your game a reality.

As we saw in the three chapters on the pedagogic theory underpinning the use of digital games for learning, there are strong links between certain types of game and constructivist learning theory. I firmly believe that it is in this area – the development of higher level skills such as evaluation, critical thinking, synthesis and analysis – that games have the most potential in higher education. Although there are also applications in memorization and development of knowledge and skills, and games clearly have a role to play there, I feel that if we ignore their potential as active learning environments we are missing most of what they have to offer.

I explored what I mean by a digital game for learning, using an open definition; many researchers have written a great deal about the definition of games, and I'm not convinced that seeking a definition in itself is useful. By adopting an inclusive definition it is possible to look at a whole range of game-like activities for learning, rather than excluding something valuable because it is 'not a game'.

I feel that in the arena of higher education in particular the acceptability of digital game-based learning is a key – and often overlooked – issue. Too much attention is often given to the perceived motivational benefits without consideration of pedagogic appropriateness. It is crucial that when using digital games for learning in this context, the educational rationale is clear, and communicated to the students: the game has to be the most effective and appropriate way to teach and learn.

A further pedagogic issue is that of the novelty value of computer games, both for teachers and learners. Any teaching innovation may be interesting for its own sake, but it is only once digital game-based learning becomes established and widespread, and we have the benefits of studies carried out over time, that we will be able to see what the effect of novelty is.

The second three chapters focused on the practical issues of using game-based learning in higher education. Unfortunately there is no single game-based solution that will work for all disciplines, but a number of factors – such as the profiles of the students, the nature of the subject discipline, the experience of the teacher and the scope for designing the course – will influence how it can be implemented. While guidelines have been provided for good practice, it is important to think of them critically rather than as absolutes, as some may not be appropriate in a given situation.

It is important that you think about game-based learning as you would any other educational innovation or modification of course design, and consider how it will fit within the procedures and regulations of the institution. The different models of integration of digital games into a course will be appropriate for different circumstances.

The assessment of digital game-based learning is another key issue, and it is important to ensure that any assessment is appropriate and valid. The introduction of game-based learning is a good opportunity to think about the way in which a course is assessed and to try new approaches. As in all aspects of introduction of a teaching innovation, evaluation is important to ensure that your practice is effective and to improve the way that teaching, learning and assessment is carried out.

The next three chapters of the book focused on the different technologies that can be used to implement digital games, and I have tried to provide an overview without expecting you to become in any way expert in a specific technology. It is likely that many people will never develop games for themselves, but hopefully these chapters will have given you an overview of the options and technologies available. The website that accompanies the book provides up-to-date links to more technical detail and to the development products discussed. The final chapter in this section has also, I hope, given you an idea of where I think the real potential for digital games for learning lies in higher education in the coming years.

These chapters aimed to provide an insight into whether you want to find an existing game (and how to evaluate it) or to develop one from scratch (there are also links to many online games sites on the website). Whichever option you go for, using digital game-based learning is never going to be easy. Introducing any innovation into higher education will be met by people who are not willing to change, systems that don't accommodate, and technology that doesn't work as expected; and learning with computer games won't work for everyone. However, hopefully this book has enthused you to start investigating the potential of digital game-based learning in your teaching.

Areas for Future Research

While there is some experimental evidence that computer games increase motivation for both children (e.g. Squire & Barab, 2004) and adults (e.g. Ebner & Holzinger, 2006) and can be an effective way to enhance learning (e.g. Kambouri et al., 2006; Hämäläinen et al., 2006), much of the research into game-based learning is anecdotal and small-scale or does not directly address issues of educational effectiveness. I feel that there is a need, also identified among policy-makers, for more robust and larger scale empirical research to provide evidence of how educational computer games can be used most effectively to teach in all areas of education (de Freitas, 2007). Mitchell and Savill-Smith, in their comprehensive review of the literature on games for learning, conclude that:

> the literature base is relatively sparse, findings often conflict in their outcomes, there is a lack of studies regarding educational games use by adolescents, some studies have methodological problems, and longitudinal studies are needed.
>
> (Mitchell & Savill-Smith, 2005: 61)

In order for digital game-based learning to be accepted within the academic community, it is important that it does not fall off the research agenda, and that we continue to question and evaluate our practice in the field. There are a number of directions for future research in games in higher education that interest me in particular: the potential for evaluating large-scale development and implementation of game-based learning; the use of in-depth qualitative investigative techniques and large-scale quantitative studies; investigation into the perception of three-dimensional environments; research into novel and experimental interface designs; and the potential for the design of asynchronous games for use in virtual learning environments to support distance learners.

Large-Scale Development and Implementation

One of the limitations of much of the research into game-based learning in higher education is that it is small-scale. An obvious future direction for research is to implement digital game-based learning on a larger scale, for example its use across a unit or programme built around a game-based environment, or delivered in an immersive game-like environment, which would enable a more rigorous evaluation of the effects on learning over time. In particular, such work would enable effects arising because of the novelty factors associated with game-based learning to be evaluated. There is great potential for collaborative gaming environments to support social interaction and group work in a range of contexts and situations with a range of students. There is also scope for evaluating a range of related issues such as the organizational and managerial issues associated with implementing a change in teaching such as this in the higher education context; technical and software design issues for supporting larger scale multi-user interaction across local and distributed networks; and teaching and learning issues such as appropriate ways to assess game-based learning courses.

Qualitative and Quantitative Evaluation

A second limitation of much research in the field of digital games for learning in higher education is its focus on a single data collection method and analysis technique, which means that it is either limited in the collection of rich and in-depth qualitative data or in quantitative evidence. A second area for future research would be to undertake more mixed-method studies, combining qualitative explorative work in the field of game-based learning, with more robust and rigorous quantitative research: for example, ethnographic investigations into virtual gaming communities or a larger phenomenographic study into the ways in which people perceive computer games in higher education, looking at different populations of individuals to discover the factors that make games appropriate for learning in different student populations, in terms of, say, subject, age, gender and previous experience with computer games; coupled with examination of evidence of the link between engagement and learning and comparative experimental designs using a control group. Although there is an intuitive link between engagement in an activity and learning from it, there is little research evidence detailing the nature or extent of the relationship. Correlation of measures of learning and measures of engagement using the same group of learners in future studies would allow this relationship to be explored in greater detail and provide empirical evidence of the extent to which increased engagement is related to increased learning. This type of rich qualitative research coupled with quantitative analysis would make an attempt to better understand the nature of game-based learning from the perspectives of the range of individuals that are involved in the phenomenon. Qualitative analysis of this sort would also enable the investigation of more sensitive topics of study relating to games and game-playing such as game addiction, the link between aggression and certain types of game, and gender roles and stereotyping in gaming environments. There is a clear need for empirical studies that provide real evidence of learning with games so that traditional teaching models can be compared with new learning methods, in order to get a true picture of the educational value of innovations.

Three-Dimensional Environments

A small number of users I've encountered in my own research appear to find it particularly difficult to navigate in three-dimensional virtual environments. It should be possible to undertake further research in this area to examine the links between visual awareness and spatial perception and to consider ways in which three-dimensional interfaces could be adapted to support navigation and, in particular, users with less experience of them. It would also be interesting to examine the cause and effect relationship: do some individuals not play three-dimensional games because of a lack of spatial ability or do they have less well-developed spatial abilities because they play fewer computer games of this type? If the latter, then there would be strong evidence for the acquisition of spatial skills through gaming.

Interaction Devices

A fourth area of interest for future research would be to consider alternative methods of interaction between game interfaces and players, with a particular focus on investigating the emerging range of interface devices used on console games machines, for example dance mats, microphones, and controllers that are sensitive to movement. This would enable consideration of the development of games for learning physical skills and provide games that would appeal to people who are motivated to play games for the physical challenge.

Future research in this area could also examine the range of ways that individuals in collaborative virtual environments could be represented, how they could interact with a range of different devices, and the methods of interaction with other people who are present in the environment. Issues of accessibility are particularly relevant here, as the use of game-based learning environments may create an inequitable experience for those learners with less experience or with physical or cognitive disabilities.

Asynchronous Collaboration

The majority of collaborative multi-user games feature synchronous communication; however, this mode would not always be practical, particularly in online or distance education where students are not necessarily online at the same time. A final area for possible future research is in the development of asynchronous games, which could provide more flexibility for the students. Issues for potential study include the design of game play for an asynchronous environment, and ways of ensuring and testing engagement over time.

There are many potential areas of future research in the field of game-based learning and the five discussed here only provide some examples of areas in which I have a particular interest. This field is one in which the amount of interest and research is fast increasing and it is hoped that the work presented here will be of use to other researchers by providing a sound theoretical and pedagogic underpinning for the use of game-based learning in higher education as well as practical tools for supporting and evaluating future research in the discipline.

Challenges for Learning with Digital Games

Although I am convinced that digital games can provide an innovative and engaging tool for learning in higher education, I am also aware that there are challenges that practitioners have to address. In this final section I will briefly review the challenges and conclude with my thoughts for the future. A major practical issue in the use of computer games for learning is how to design and develop the educational game to be used; whether to use off-the-shelf games software designed for entertainment, or to create bespoke educational games. The problems associated with the design of bespoke education software often involve the amount of money spent on producing it compared to entertainment software, and how this affects the expectations of learners. Jenkins (2002) argues that most educational software is of poor quality, badly edited and unprofessional. It will never be the case, however, that the amounts of money spent on commercial software will be available for education, and it is more important that resources be used to ensure that educational games are well designed in terms of playability and learning. The growing trend towards modifying existing games software for use in education (de Freitas, 2007) may provide one way to address this issue.

Other criticisms of game-based learning include that transfer of game-based learning to real life may not be clear (e.g. Dempsey *et al.*, 1993–4), particularly in the context of the higher level skills discussed in this book. Motivation to play a game may actually be detrimental to learning (e.g. Jacques *et al.*, 1995) and games may be a less efficient manner of learning than traditional methods, not least because of the amount of time that is required to become proficient at the game, time that could be used for learning (e.g. Alessi & Trollip, 2001).

Some of the other disadvantages associated with computer game-based learning include that it is often difficult to pitch games at the right level of interest and challenge for their intended users, they can be gender-specific, often have violent or stereotypical characters, and many computer games are designed as single player whereas collaboration and group work can dramatically enhance learning (Becta, 2001). In addition, there is evidence that using game-based learning may discriminate against women and may lead to aggressive, addictive or anti-social behaviours (Sandford & Williamson, 2005), although this is less of an issue in relation to adult game-playing, particularly where game use is short-term and regulated. Games may be impractical for use in a classroom setting because of time constraints and the time taken for teaching staff to learn and support them (Becta, 2001), and there may be a lack of available equipment (de Freitas, 2007) and technical infrastructure. There are issues with ensuring alignment between games outcomes, learning outcomes and assessment (Sandford et al., 2006; Lean et al., 2006). Jones (1997) argues that, while games and simulations can be powerful learning tools, they can also damage personal relationships and cause emotional hurt and distress.

Despite the disadvantages and practical implementation issues, it is clear that certain types of computer game do have the power to engage certain types of people. If games can be designed to encapsulate sound learning principles of interactive and collaborative experimentation as well as learning content that is appropriate to the curriculum and assessment, then I feel that they can clearly be an appropriate tool for learning. Whether they are the most appropriate and acceptable to learners will depend upon the particular learning context in which they are used.

It is my hope that in the future digital games will be used more widely and more creatively in higher education so that a body of evidence about what is established good practice can be created and shared among the community. I will also reiterate the importance of ongoing systematic and robust research into the use of games so that we can fully understand their benefits and drawbacks. I hope that after reading this book you will appreciate the pedagogic benefits of using digital games – pragmatically and creatively – in higher education and be enthused to try out some of the ideas presented here for yourself.

Glossary

Alternate reality game (ARG)   Narrative-based game that unfolds over time combining elements of the real and online worlds and presenting ongoing challenges for the players to solve collaboratively as the plot is revealed.

Avatar   A representation of the user (usually graphical) in a game or virtual world.

Chat room   Multi-user virtual space in which two or more users can communicate with one another using text (and sometime limited graphics) in real-time.

Commercial off-the-shelf (COTS) games   Games that can be bought from a computer or game shop and are designed purely for fun and entertainment rather than for learning. Community forum   Asynchronous discussion forum that members of a community can use to post messages and talk to one another on a one-to-many basis.

Community forum   Asynchronous discussion forum that members of a community can use to post messages and talk to one another on a one-to-manybasis.

Constructive alignment   A designed and deliberate mapping between learning objectives (or outcomes), learning activities and assessment.

Constructivism   A group of theories that generally conceive learning as a process whereby learners construct their own understandings and meanings from active experience in authentic contexts and validate them through interaction with others.

Engagement   Complete concentration and focus, immersion, and emotional captivation in an activity.

Instant messaging Computer-to-computer networking software that allows users to send messages directly from one computer to another in real-time.

Interactive fiction (IF) Text-based environments that use commands to control characters, influence the environment and progress the story. This includes the text adventure games that were popular in the 1980s but there are also examples of interactive fiction with more literary emphasis, where the focus is on the narrative and writing rather than puzzle-solving.

Leader board A list of players who participate in a game ordered by some criteria (usually score) so that players can see how well they are faring against others.

Massively multi-player online role-playing game (MMORPG) A networked computer game where large numbers of players interact and collaborate in a virtual fantasy world, undertaking quests, fighting enemies and exploring the environment. Popular examples include *World of Warcraft*, *Guild Wars* and *RuneScape*.

Mini-game Smaller game contained within a larger game that is secondary to the main game play.

Mobile game Game that is played on a handheld mobile device such as a phone.

Modding Making modifications or extensions to an existing commercial game (usually with creation software provided by the game manufacturer).

Multi-user virtual environment (MUVE) Online virtual world in which large numbers of users can simultaneously navigate the virtual space, interact with objects and communicate with one another.

Rich media Electronic or online media that are typically interactive and use multiple media types.

Second Life One of the most famous online immersive virtual worlds, developed by Linden Lab. Users are represented by graphical characters (called avatars) and can talk (either with text or voice) and interact with other users, navigate through the locations of the world, as well as building objects and environments themselves.

Social networking Websites or software that allow users to create personal profiles, share details about themselves and join networks and groups of users.

Virtual learning environment (VLE) Web-based software that provides a single point of access to a range of tools to support learning, such as teaching materials, means of communication and assessments.

Walkthrough Step-by-step guide to how to complete a game, usually posted online by someone who has already completed it.

References

Alessi, S. M. & Trollip, S. R. (2001). *Multimedia for Learning*. Boston: Allyn & Bacon.

Anderson, L.W., & Krathwohl, D. R. (Eds) (2001). *A Taxonomy for Learning, Teaching, and Assessing: A Revision of Bloom's Taxonomy of Educational Objectives*. New York: Longman.

Bateman, C. (Ed.) (2007). *Game Writing: Narrative Skills for Videogames*. Boston, MA: Charles River Media.

Becta (2001). Computer games in education project: findings report. Retrieved Jan. 2009 from http://partners.becta.org.uk/index.php?section=rh&rid=13595

Bennett, S., Maton, K. & Kervin, L. (2008). The 'digital natives' debate: a critical review of the evidence. *British Journal of Educational Technology*, 39(5), 775–86.

Benyon, D., Turner, P. & Turner, S. (2005). *Designing Interactive Systems*. Harlow: Addison-Wesley.

Biggs, J. (2003). *Teaching for Quality Learning at University* (2nd edn). Maidenhead: Open University Press.

Biggs, W. D. (1993). Using supplementary activities with computerized business simulations to develop transferable skills. In S. Lodge, F. Percival & D. Saunders (Eds), *The Simulation and Gaming Yearbook*, vol. 1: *Developing Transferable Skills in Education and Training*. London: Kogan Page.

Bloom, B. S. (1956). *Taxonomy of Educational Objectives*, Handbook 1: *The Cognitive Domain*. New York: David McKay Co. Inc.

Boud, D. & Feletti, G. (1991). *The Challenge of Problem Based Learning*. London: Kogan Page.

Bredemeir, M. E. & Greenblat, C. E. (1981). The educational effectiveness of games: a synthesis of findings. *Simulation & Games*, 12(3), 307–32.

Bruner, J. S. (1966). *Toward a Theory of Instruction*. Oxford: Oxford University Press.

Caillois, R. (2001). *Man, Play and Games*. New York: Free Press.

Chapman, E. (2003). Alternative approaches to assessing student engagement rates. *Practical Assessment, Research & Evaluation*, 8(13). Retrieved Jan. 2009 from http://pareonline.net/getvn.asp?v=8&n=13.

Childress, M. D. & Braswell, R. (2006). Using massively multiplayer online role-playing games for online learning. *Distance Education*, 27(2), 187–96.

CIBER (2008). *Information Behaviour of the Researcher of the Future*. Bristol: JISC.

Colarusso, C. A. (1993). Play in adulthood. *Psychoanalytic Study of the Child*, 48, 225–45.

Connolly, T., Stansfield, M. & Hainey, T. (2008). Development of a general framework for evaluating games-based learning. In T. Connolly and M. Stansfield (Eds), *Proceedings of the 2nd European Conference on Game-Based Learning*. Reading: Academic Conferences Ltd.

Cooper, P. A. (1993). Paradigm shifts in designed instruction: from behaviorism to cognitivism to constructivism. *Educational Technology*, 33(5), 12–19.

Crawford, C. (1984). *The Art of Computer Game Design*. Berkeley, CA: Osborne/McGraw Hill. Retrieved May 19, 2009 from http://www.vancouver.wsu.edu/fac/peabody/game-book/Coverpage.html.

Csikszentmihalyi, M. (2002). *Flow: The Psychology of Happiness*. London: Random House.

Dansky, R. (2007). Introduction to game narrative. In C. Bateman (Ed.), *Game Writing: Narrative Skills for Videogames*. Boston, MA: Charles River Media.

de Freitas, S. I. (2006). Using games and simulations for supporting learning. *Learning, Media and Technology*, 31(4), 343–58.

de Freitas, S. (2007). *Learning in Immersive Worlds: A Review of Game-Based Learning*. Bristol: JISC.

de Freitas, S., Savill-Smith, C. & Attewell, J. (2006). *Computer Games and Simulations for Adult Learning: Case Studies from Practice*. London: Learning and Skills Network.

Dempsey, J., Lucassen, B., Gilley, W. & Rasmussen, K. (1993–4). Since Malone's theory of intrinsically motivating instruction: What's the score in the gaming literature? *Journal of Educational Technology Systems*, 22(2), 173–183.

Dempsey, J. V., Haynes, L. L., Lucassen, B. A. & Casey, M. S. (2002). Forty simple computer games and what they could mean to educators. *Simulation & Gaming*, 33(2), 157–68.

Densombe, M. (2002). *Ground Rules for Good Research: A 10 Point Guide for Social Researchers*. Maidenhead: Open University Press.

Dormans, J. (2008). Beyond iconic simulation. Paper presented at 'Gaming 2008: Designing for Engaging Experience and Social Interaction', Amsterdam, 22–27 July.

Draper, S. (1999). Analysing fun as a candidate software requirement. *Personal Technology*, 3, 117–22.

Ducheneaut, N. & Moore, R. J. (2005). More than just 'XP': learning social skills in massively multiplayer online games. *Interactive Technology & Smart Education*, 2, 89–100.

Ebner, M. & Holzinger, A. (2007). Successful implementation of user-centered game based learning in higher education: an example from civil engineering. *Computers and Education*, 49(3), 873–90.

Ellington, H., Addinall, E. & Percival, F. (1982). *A Handbook of Game Design*. London: Kogan Page.

Facer, K., Joiner, R., Stanton, D., Reidz, J., Hullz, R. & Kirk, D. (2004). Savannah: mobile gaming and learning? *Journal of Computer-Assisted Learning*, 20, 399–409.

Feinstein, A. H., Mann, S. & Corsun, D, L. (2002). Charting the experiential territory: clarifying definitions and uses of computer simulation, games and role play. *Journal of Management Development*, 21(10), 732–44.

Gagné, R. M., Briggs, L. J. & Wager, W. W. (1992). *Principles of Instructional Design*. Fort Worth, TX: Harcourt Brace & Co.

Gee, J. P. (2003). *What Video Games Have to Teach us about Learning and Literacy*. New York: Palgrave Macmillan.

Grabinger, S., Dunlap, J. & Duffield, J. (1997). Rich environments for active learning. *ALT-J*, 5(2), 5–17.

Greco, M. & Murgia, G. (2007). Improving negotiation skills through an online business game. In D. Remenyi (Ed.), *Proceedings of the European Conference on Game-Based Learning*. Reading: Academic Conferences Ltd.

Gredler, M. (1996). Educational games and simulations: a technology in search of a (research) paradigm. In D. Jonassen (Ed.), *Handbook of Research for Educational Communications and Technology*. New York: Macmillan.

Hämäläinen, R., Manninen, T., Järvelä, S. & Häkkinen, P. (2006). Learning to collaborate: designing collaboration in a 3-D game environment. *The Internet and Higher Education*, 9, 47–61.

Harvey, J. (Ed.) (1998). *Evaluation Cookbook*. Edinburgh: Heriot-Watt University.

Hodson, P., Connolly, M. & Saunders, D. (2001). Can computer-based learning support adult learners? *Journal of Further and Higher Education*, 25(3), 325–35.

Hollins, P. & Robbins, S. (2008). Educational affordances of multi-user virtual environments. In D. Heider (Ed.), *Living Virtually: Researching New Worlds*. New York: Peter Lang Publishing.

Hon, A. (2005). The rise of ARGs. *Gamasutra*. Retrieved Jan. 2009 from http://gamasutra.com/features/20050509/hon_01.shtml

Honebein, P. C. (1996). Seven goals for the design of constructivist learning environments. In B. G. Wilson (Ed.), *Constructivist Learning Environments: Case Studies in Instructional Design*. Englewood Cliffs, NJ: Educational Technology Publications.

Houser, R. & Deloach, S. (1998). Learning from games: seven principles of effective design. *Technical Communication* (third quarter), 319–29.

Hughey, L. M. (2002). A pilot study investigating visual methods of measuring engagement during e-learning. Report produced by the Learning Lab at the Center for Applied Research in Educational Technologies (CARET), University of Cambridge.

Huizenga, J., Admiraal, W., Akkerman, S. & ten Dam, G. (2008). Cognitive and affective effects of learning history by playing a mobile game. In T. Connolly and M. Stansfield (Eds), *Proceedings of the 2nd European Conference on Game-Based Learning*. Reading: Academic Conferences Ltd.

IPSOS MORI. (2007). *Student Expectations Study*. Bristol: JISC.

Jacques, R., Preece, J. & Carey, T. (1995). Engagement as a design concept for multimedia. *Canadian Journal of Educational Communication*, 24(1), 49–59.

Jenkins, H. (2002). Game theory. *Technology Review*, 29 March.

Johnson, S. & Johnson, D. W. (1989). *Cooperation and Competition: Theory and Research*. Edina, MN: Interaction Book Co.

Jones, K. (1997). Damage caused by simulation/games. In B. Cox, D. Saunders and P. Saunders (Eds), *The International Simulation & Gaming Yearbook*, vol. 5: *Research into Simulations in Education*. London: Kogan Page.

Kambouri, M., Thomas, S. & Mellar, H. (2006). Playing the literacy game: a case study in adult education. *Learning, Media and Technology,* 31(4), 395–410.

Kiili, K. (2005). Digital game-based learning: towards an experiential gaming model. *The Internet and Higher Education,* 8, 13–24.

Klabbers, J. H. G. (1999). Three easy pieces: a taxonomy on gaming. In D. Saunders & J. Severn (Eds), *The International Simulation & Gaming Yearbook,* vol. 7: *Simulations and Games for Strategy and Policy Planning.* London: Kogan Page.

Knowles, M. (1998). *The Adult Learner* (5th edn). Houston, TX: Butterworth-Heinemann.

Kolb, D. A. (1984). *Experiential Learning: Experience as the Source of Learning and Development.* New Jersey, NJ: Prentice Hall.

Kolo, C. & Baur, T. (2008). *Homo Ludens* going mobile? Perspectives on mobile gaming. Paper presented at 'Gaming 2008: Designing for Engaging Experience and Social Interaction', Amsterdam, 22–27 July.

Koster, R. (2005). *A Theory of Fun for Game Design.* Scottsdale, AZ: Paragylph Press.

Krawczyk, M. & Novak, J. (2006). *Game Development Essentials: Game Story and Character Development.* Clifton Park, NY: Delmar Learning.

Land, S. M. & Hannafin, M. J. 2000. Student-centered learning environments. In D. H. Jonassen & S. M. Land (Eds), *Theoretical Foundations of Learning Environments.* Mahwah, NJ: Lawrence Erlbaum Associates.

Lave, J. & Wenger, E. (1991). *Situated Learning: Legitimate Peripheral Participation.* Cambridge: Cambridge University Press.

Lean, J., Moizer, J., Towler, M. & Abbey, C. (2006). Simulations and games: use and barriers in higher education. *Active Learning in Higher Education,* 7(3), 227–43.

Lepper, M. R. & Malone, T. W. 1987. Intrinsic motivation and instructional effectiveness in computer-based education. In R. Snow and M. Farr (Eds), *Aptitude, Learning and Instruction,* vol. 3: *Cognitive and Affective Process Analysis.* Hillside, NJ: Lawrence Erlbaum Associates.

Livingstone, D. (2007). Learning support in multi-user virtual environments. In D. Remenyi (Ed.), *Proceedings of the European Conference on Game-Based Learning.* Reading: Academic Conferences Ltd.

Malone, T. (1980). *What Makes Things Fun to Learn? A Study of Intrinsically Motivating Computer Games.* Technical Report CIS-7. Palo Alto, CA: Xerox Parc.

Malone, T. & Lepper, M. R. (1987). Making learning fun: a taxonomy of intrinsic motivations for learning. In R. E. Snow & M. J. Farr (Eds), *Aptitude, Learning and Instruction,* vol. 3: *Cognitive and Affective Process Analysis.* Hillsdale, NJ: Erlbaum.

McConnell, D. (2000). *Implementing Computer Supported Cooperative Learning* (2nd edn). London: Kogan Page.

McConnell, D. (2006). *E-learning Groups and Communities.* Milton Keynes: Open University Press.

Magnussen, R. (2005). Learning games as a platform for simulated science practice. Paper presented at the Digital Games Research Association 2005 Conference, Vancouver, Canada.

Mitchell, A. & Savill-Smith, C. (2005). *The Use of Computer and Video Games for Learning: A Review of the Literature.* London: Learning and Skills Development Agency.

Montfort, N. (2005). *Twisty Little Passages: An Approach to Interactive Fiction.* Cambridge, MA: MIT Press.

Moseley, A. (2008). An alternative reality for higher education? Lessons to be learned from online reality games. Paper presented at ALT-C 2008, Leeds, UK.

Oblinger, D. (2004). The next generation of educational engagement. *Journal of Interactive Media in Education*, 8, 1–18.

Oxland, K. (2004). *Gameplay and Design*. Harlow: Addison-Wesley.

Pal, J. & Stubbs, M. (2002). Of mice and pen. *Learning and Teaching in Action*, 2, 11–16.

Pal, J., Stubbs, M. & Lee, A. (2005). Designing a web-driven retail marketing simulation. *Journal of Marketing Management*, 21(7/8), 835–58.

Palloff, R. M. & Pratt, K. (2003). *The Virtual Student: A Profile and Guide to Working with Online Learners*. San Francisco, CA: Jossey-Bass.

Piatt, K. (2007). *studentquest 2006 a.k.a. 'Who is Herring Hale?'*. Summary Project Report. Brighton: University of Brighton.

Pimenidis, E. (2007). Developing a computer game for university library induction. In D. Remenyi (Ed.), *Proceedings of the European Conference on Game-Based Learning*. Reading: Academic Conferences Ltd.

Prensky, M. (2001). *Digital Game-Based Learning*. New York: McGraw Hill.

Prensky, M. (2006). *Don't Bother Me Mom – I'm Learning!* St Paul, MN: Paragon House.

Read, J. C., MacFarlane, S. J. & Casey, C. (2002). Endurability, engagement, and expectations: measuring children's fun. In Becker, M. M., Markopoulos, P. & Kersten-Tsikalkina, M. (Eds) *Proceedings of Interaction Design*. Maastricht: Shaker.

Rieber, L. (1996). Seriously considering play: designing interactive learning environments based on the blending of microworlds, simulations and games. *Education and Training Resource & Development*, 44, 42–58.

Rieber, L. P., Smith, L. & Noah, D. (1998). The value of serious play. *Educational Technology*, 38(6), 29–37.

Rockler, M. (1989). The British mystery writer as simulation/gamer. *Simulation/Games for Learning*, 19(2), 63–75.

Robertson, J. & Howells, C. (2008). Computer game design: opportunities for successful learning. *Computers & Education*, 50(2), 559–78.

Robson, C. (2002). *Real World Research*. Malden, MA: Blackwell.

Rylands, T. (2007). ITC to inspire with Myst. Retrieved Jan. 2009 from http://www.timrylands.com/index.html

Salen, K. & Zimmerman, E. (2004). *Rules of Play: Game Design Fundamentals*. Cambridge, MA: MIT Press.

Sandford, R. & Williamson, B. (2005). *Games and Learning*. Bristol: Futurelab.

Sandford, R., Ulicsak, M., Facer, K. & Rudd, T. (2006). *Teaching with Games: Using Commercial Off-the-Shelf Computer Games in Formal Education*. Bristol: Futurelab.

Savery, J. R. & Duffy, T. M. (1995). Problem-based learning: an instructional model and its constructivist framework. *Educational Technology*, 35, 31–38.

Shedroff, N. (2001). *Experience Design 1*. Indianapolis, IN: New Riders.

Squire, K. D. (2005). Changing the game: what happens when videogames enter the classroom? *Innovate*, 1/6.

Squire, K. & Barab, S. (2004). Replaying history: engaging urban underserved students in learning world history through computer simulation games. Paper presented at the 6th International Conference on Learning Sciences, Santa Monica, CA.

Steinkuehler, C. A. (2004). Learning in massively multiplayer online games. Paper presented at the 6th International Conference on Learning Sciences, Santa Monica, CA.

Stewart, S. (2006). Alternate reality games. Retrieved Jan. 2009 from http://www.seanstewart.org/interactive/args/

Stubbs, M. & Pal, J. (2003). The development, design and delivery of a retail simulation. *British Journal of Educational Technology*, 34(5), 1–11.

Sung, Y-T., Chang, K-E. & Lee, M-D. (2008). Designing multimedia games for young children's taxonomic concept development. *Computers and Education*. 50(3), 1037–51.

Thiagarajan, S. (1993). How to maximise transfer from simulation games through systematic debriefing. In S. Lodge, F. Percival & D. Saunders (Eds), *The Simulation and Gaming Yearbook*, vol. 1: *Developing Transferable Skills in Education and Training*. London: Kogan Page.

Thiagarajan, S. & Jasinski, M. (2004). Virtual games for real learning: a seriously fun way to learn online. ITFORUM Paper #41. Retrieved Jan. 2009 from http://it.coe.uga.edu/itforum/paper41/paper41.html

Virvou, M., Katsionis, G. & Manos, K. (2004). On the motivation and attractiveness scope of the virtual reality user interface of an educational game. Paper presented at the 4th International Conference on Computer Science, Krakow, Poland.

Vygotsky, L. (1978). *Mind in Society: The Development of Higher Psychological Functions*. Cambridge, MA: Harvard University Press.

Whitton, N. (2007). An investigation into the potential of collaborative computer games to support learning in higher education. Doctoral thesis. Edinburgh: Napier University School of Computing. Retrieved Sept. 2008 from http://playthinklearn.net/?page_id=8.

Whitton, N. & Hynes, N. (2006). Evaluating the effectiveness of an online simulation to teach business skills. *E-Journal of Instructional Science and Technology*, 9(1). Retrieved Jan. 2009 from http://www.ascilite.org.au/ajet/e-jist/docs/vol9_no1/papers/current_practice/whitton_hynes.htm.

Whitton, N., Jones, R., Whitton, P. & Wilson, S. (2008). Innovative induction with alternate reality games. In T. Connolly and M. Stansfield (Eds), *Proceedings of the 2nd European Conference on Games-Based Learning*. Reading: Academic Conferences Ltd.

Wier, K. & Baranowski, M. (2008). Simulating history to understand international politics. *Simulation & Gaming*. Retrieved Jan. 2009 from http://sg/sagepub/com/

Wilson, B. G. (1996). What is a constructivist learning environment? In B. G. Wilson (Ed.), *Constructivist Learning Environments: Case Studies in Instructional Design*. Englewood Cliffs, NJ: Educational Technology Publications.

Wittgenstein, L. (1976). *Philosophical Investigations* (3rd edn). Oxford: Basil Blackwell.

Wolf, M. J. P. (2001). Genre and the video game. In M. J. P. Wolf (Ed.), *The Medium of the Video Game* (113–34). Austin, TX: University of Texas Press.

Index

CONTENTS